Mission

YOUR PART IN GOD'S PLAN FOR THE NATIONS

by Alan Purser

thegoodbook
COMPANY

To Luke, Katie, Jacob, Reuben and Sam
Psalm 67:1-2

Mission
The Good Book Guide to Mission
© Alan Purser/The Good Book Company, 2019
Series Consultants: Tim Chester, Tim Thornborough, Carl Laferton, Anne Woodcock

Published by:
The Good Book Company

thegoodbook.com | thegoodbook.co.uk
thegoodbook.com.au | thegoodbook.co.nz | thegoodbook.co.in

Unless indicated, all Scripture references are taken from the Holy Bible, New International Version. Copyright © 2011 Biblica. Used by permission.

A CIP catalogue record for this book is available from the British Library.

ISBN: 9781784983628 | Printed in Turkey

Design by André Parker

CONTENTS

Introduction: Good Book Guides

Every Bible-study group is different—yours may take place in a church building, in a home or in a cafe, on a train, over a leisurely mid-morning coffee or squashed into a 30-minute lunch break. Your group may include new Christians, mature Christians, non-Christians, mums and tots, students, businessmen or teens. That's why we've designed these *Good Book Guides* to be flexible for use in many different situations.

Our aim in each session is to uncover the meaning of a passage, and see how it fits into the "big picture" of the Bible. But that can never be the end. We also need to appropriately apply what we have discovered to our lives. Let's take a look at what is included:

⊕ **Talkabout:** Most groups need to "break the ice" at the beginning of a session, and here's the question that will do that. It's designed to get people talking around a subject that will be covered in the course of the Bible study.

⊕ **Investigate:** The Bible text for each session is broken up into manageable chunks, with questions that aim to help you understand what the passage is about. **The Leader's Guide** contains **guidance on questions**, and sometimes ⊗ additional "follow-up" questions.

⊕ **Explore more (optional):** These questions will help you connect what you have learned to other parts of the Bible, so you can begin to fit it all together like a jig-saw; or occasionally look at a part of the passage that's not dealt with in detail in the main study.

⊖ **Apply:** As you go through a Bible study, you'll keep coming across **apply** sections. These are questions to get the group discussing what the Bible teaching means in practice for you and your church. ⊡ **Getting personal** is an opportunity for you to think, plan and pray about the changes that you personally may need to make as a result of what you have learned.

⊕ **Pray:** We want to encourage prayer that is rooted in God's word—in line with His concerns, purposes and promises. So each session ends with an opportunity to review the truths and challenges highlighted by the Bible study, and turn them into prayers of request and thanksgiving.

The **Leader's Guide** and introduction provide historical background information, explanations of the Bible texts for each session, ideas for **optional extra** activities, and guidance on how best to help people uncover the truths of God's word.

Why study mission?

Mission is the heartbeat of the Bible. From the time of Adam and Eve's rebellion until the promised new heaven and new earth, God is on a mission: to call rebellious people into a reconciled relationship with him.

God's plan to bring salvation to the ends of the earth was spelled out by his prophets in the Old Testament and proclaimed by his apostles in the New Testament.

At the centre of this mission plan is God's anointed Saviour King, the Lord Jesus Christ: it is Jesus who makes atonement for sin and who brings in the kingdom of God.

These seven studies chart the unfolding of God's plan for mission in the Scriptures. To select just seven passages that capture the Bible's teaching on mission necessitates difficult choices, with the omission of some passages that might appear rather more obvious candidates for inclusion! However, taken together, these studies provide an introduction to a biblical theology of mission. As such, they are a window into the mind and heart of God, enabling us to sense his loving concern for those who have rebelled against him, to appreciate his gracious gift in the person of Christ and to understand how his mission continues in today's world.

These studies are also an invitation for believers to share his passion for the lost and to align our priorities with his, until Christ returns. God is doing something tremendously exciting in our world, and he invites us to be part of it. As you study the topic of mission through the Bible, you'll be spurred on to engage in mission in your local area; and you'll be better equipped to support and pray for the work of mission in other cities and countries.

As you begin these studies, pray that they would awaken in you a fresh grasp of God's mission, and a renewed engagement in his plan for the nations.

1

Isaiah 66:18-24
IT'S GOD'S MISSION

⊕ talkabout

1. Imagine you are part of the planning team for a mission to Mars. You've been charged with explaining the plan to the media. What would you want to communicate? What questions would you anticipate being asked?

⊕ investigate

The Old Testament prophets were insiders on God's mission plan, and spoke clearly about it. Writing 800 years before Christ, Isaiah was God's spokesman to the nation of Judah, pronouncing judgment on his people's sin, but also declaring good news of a coming Saviour whose righteous rule will last for ever. These twin themes (judgment and salvation) run throughout the book and find their fulfilment in the person of God's chosen servant, who will "bring salvation to the ends of the earth" (Isaiah 49:6). Isaiah's prophecy finishes with a majestic vision of God's agenda for mission.

❯ Read Isaiah 66:18-21

2. What precisely is the mission for which the time has arrived (v 18, see also the end of v 19)?

> ### DICTIONARY
> **Glory (v 18):** God's awesome, majestic weightiness.
> **Grain offerings (v 20):** a gift of grain to acknowledge God's provision.
> **Levites (v 21):** the tribe within Israel responsible for serving in the temple.

• Who is ultimately responsible for it?

- What is the scope of this mission?

- What is the fruit of this mission?

In verses 19-20 we see that God's mission will be carried out in two stages.

3. What is the first stage of God's mission plan (v 19a)?

- **Read Isaiah 7:14 and Matthew 1:22-23.** Who is this "sign"?

- **Read John 12:32-33.** What in particular about this "sign" will draw people in?

4. What is the second stage of God's mission plan (Isaiah 66:19b)?

• Who will proclaim this message, and where will it be taken?

• Where will these people be gathered to, and what will they do (v 20-21)?

⊡ getting personal

Have you ever considered that you are a resident of a "distant island" that at one time had "not heard of [God's] fame"? Pause to give thanks to God for those who first brought the gospel to your country—and for any individual or group who opened up the message of salvation for you.

⊖ apply

5. What are some of the implications of knowing that...

• all mission is God's mission?

• the fruit of mission is the church?

⬇ investigate

❯ Read Isaiah 66:22-24

DICTIONARY

Sabbath (v 23):
Saturday; the Jewish
holy day of rest.

6. What is the ultimate goal of God's mission (v 22, and also v 18-21)?

7. What would spoil "the new heavens and the new earth"? How does this account for the grotesque vision with which Isaiah finishes?

⊡ explore more

optional

Towards the end of the Bible we read again of "a new heaven and a new earth":

❯ Read Revelation 21:1-8

What similarities do you see between this passage and Isaiah's closing vision?

Why is such a terrible judgment necessary in order for God's glory to be established?

What ought this knowledge prompt us to do? (See Mark 9:42-49 for an example.)

➔ apply

8. The ultimate goal of God's mission is his glory. How do your goals stack up against his? What difference would adopting God's goal make when it comes to world mission?

9. Often we look at the scale and evil of suffering, injustice and oppression in the world and ask, "What on earth is God doing?" What is the answer to that question, according to this passage?

⊡ getting personal

Consider where you fit in to the agenda for mission set out in this passage. How do your ambitions in life fit with Isaiah's vision of the future? Is there any action you will take as a result of this study?

⬆ pray

In the light of this vision, what ought we to be asking God to do? Pray for...

• yourself: that your goals and motives would increasingly line up with God's goals and motives.

• your church: for a common mind around a Bible-driven understanding of mission, and unity in the marshalling of resources for mission. Ask God to give you a fresh impetus for mission beyond the local area (or perhaps cross culturally within your locality).

• the world: which countries today are equivalent to those "distant islands who have not heard of his fame or seen his glory"? Bring them before God in prayer, and ask him to send out labourers especially into those parts of his harvest field (Matthew 8:38).

2 Luke 19:1-10
A RICH MAN MADE POOR?

The story so far

God is on a mission to gather a people for himself from every nation and to establish his glory. It's his mission!

⊕ talkabout

1. The doorbell rings, and a stranger stands at the door. What kinds of questions immediately spring to mind? Assuming you felt safe to do this, what would you want to ask?

   WHat Do You WANT.
   WHo ARE You'

⊕ investigate

The Gospel-writers pose, and answer, many different questions about Jesus, but the most important ones are these: "Who is this man?" and "Why has he come?"

In Luke 19 Jesus demonstrates his answers, and gives a succinct summary statement of his mission. It is worked out in Jesus' encounter with one individual, as Luke enables us to see God's mission at work in the life of this one man.

2. Jesus is on a journey from the north of the country to the south. **Read Luke 18:31-34.** What was on his mind as he headed towards Jerusalem?

   HE WAS THINKING ABOUT HIS
   TRIAL AND HIS DEATH BECAUSE HE
   KNEW ALREADY WHAT HAD TO BE

Nevertheless, as Jesus passes through the town of Jericho, he takes time with one individual by the name of Zacchaeus.

> **Read Luke 19:1-10**

3. What kind of person was Zacchaeus? What are we told about him in verses 1-4?

> HE WAS A TAX COLLECTOR
> HE WANTED TO KNOW
> WHAT JESUS WAS

DICTIONARY

Abraham (v 9): the man chosen by God to be the forefather of the whole Jewish nation (Genesis 12 – 25).

The Son of Man (v 10): Jesus (a title taken from a prophecy in Daniel 7:13-14).

4. In 19:5-7 Jesus' words to Zacchaeus bring two very different reactions—one from Zacchaeus and one from the crowd. How would you describe each of these? What would be the probable reason for each?

> HE WAS HAPPY TO TAKE JESUS
> HOME WITH HIM,
> BUT THE CROWN THOUGHT ZACCAES
> A SINER SO. HE SHOULD NOT GO THERE

At that time, Palestine was subject to taxation by the occupying Roman forces, administrated using locally appointed tax officials. As a chief tax collector, Zacchaeus was in charge of a team whose task was to enforce the tax laws on their fellow Jews—in return the tax collectors generally kept a portion of the "take". It was not a coincidence that Zacchaeus was a wealthy man—nor a surprise that he was loathed by his compatriots!

5. We're not told much about the conversation that Jesus and Zacchaeus had in Zacchaeus' home. But we are told about Zacchaeus' response. How would you sum it up?

> BY MEETING JESUS HE CHANGED
> HIS MIND ABOUT KEEPING THE PROFITS
> GIVING IT BACK TO THE POOR

• What might Jesus have said to provoke this response, do you think?

> DO UNTO OTHER AS YOU WOULD
> BE DONE BY

- Imagine you are Zacchaeus' financial advisor: how might you describe his decision?!

YOU WOULD THINK HE WAS BEING FOOLISH

- Why did Zacchaeus choose not to follow any "sensible" advice, do you think? (What is implied by the manner in which Zacchaeus addresses Jesus?)

HE HUMBLED HIS SELF IN FRONT OF JESUS.

⊡ explore more

Jesus' brief stay in Jericho resulted in a notoriously rich man being made poor. Consider how this fits with Jesus' mission as set out at the beginning of his public ministry in the synagogue in Nazareth.

▶ **Read Luke 4:16-21**

In this incident, sometimes called the "Nazareth Manifesto", Jesus takes the well-known messianic description of Isaiah 61:1-2 and applies the words to himself.

Which verb is repeated three times in the passage? How does this explain the prominence of preaching in Jesus' public ministry?

How does this help us understand what is meant by the descriptions of people in the Nazareth Manifesto?

The first thing Jesus says that he has come to do is to "proclaim good news to the poor". How has this played out in Jericho in chapter 19?

6. Jesus' reaction to Zacchaeus' response is extremely positive. What precisely does Jesus say has happened?

THE RICH TAX COLLECTOR DOSE A TURNAROUND AND GIVE THE PROFITS BACK TO THE POOR BECAUSE HE MET JESUS

- With whom does Jesus now associate this changed tax collector? Why is that significant, do you think?

BECAUSE IT IS JESUS IS MISSION!

📖 getting personal

Jesus came to bring spiritual health and wealth to the lost, which prompts this question: has this salvation come to your house?

This story shows that it is never too late, even for the most notorious sinner—but it also teaches the necessity of responding in repentance (a radical change of mind, attitude and behaviour) and faith (which places full trust in God's gracious promise of forgiveness and a fresh start) in Jesus as Lord.

7. Looking back over this incident, would you say that this is the story of a rich man made poor? Or a poor man made rich? What difference does this distinction make?

HE MIGHT BE POORER IN MONE BUT MUCH RICHER IN SPIRIT AND MORE GENEROUS.

8. Verse 10 is Jesus' great declaration of the purpose for which he came into the world. What is it? Why do you think Jesus said this at that point?

- What would it take for Jesus to carry out his mission?

FOR ALL THE PEOPLE IN THE WORLD TO BEAUFAT IN HIM.

⊡ getting personal

Zacchaeus was healthy (he ran and climbed a tree) and wealthy (notoriously so), and yet Jesus recognised him as a poor and needy man. Addressing him by name, Jesus took him seriously, spent time with him in his home (despite the open criticism of the crowd) and led him to repentance and faith.

How does this portrait of Jesus personally encourage you?

⊡ apply

9. In what sense was Zacchaeus lost? What would it take to...

• see people as Jesus saw Zacchaeus?

• treat people as Jesus treated Zacchaeus?

10. What do Jesus' words in Luke 19:9-10 mean for how we assess poverty and wealth? Are there any implications for our understanding of the scope of mission?

11. If we've been "found" by Jesus, what would it look like to respond with the same heart as Zacchaeus?

⊡ **pray**

Pray for...

- all the "Zacchaeuses" you know among your family, friends, neighbours or work colleagues.

- your own response to Jesus, in repentance and faith.

- a growing understanding within your church of Jesus and his mission: that you might share his passion for the lost and, like him, be willing to search them out, spend time with them rather than write them off, and speak about the one who came to save them.

3 John 3:1-21
NOT WHY JESUS CAME

The story so far

God is on a mission to gather a people for himself from every nation and to establish his glory. It's his mission!

Jesus came "to seek and to save the lost" (Luke 19:10). His encounter with Zacchaeus takes us right to the heart of the difference his mission makes.

⊕ talkabout

1. Imagine a school classroom where, in the absence of the teacher, the students are in full revolt—there is shouting and banging, property is being thrown around and those unable to stand up for themselves are being bullied. The noise of what is happening reaches down the corridor to the staff room, from where the deputy head is despatched on a mission by the headteacher. Upon reaching the classroom, the deputy head throws open the door, enters and… then what?

Discuss what you think will happen next.

He ROARS AT THE CLASS TO SIT DOWN AND BE Quiet

In the last study we saw that Jesus came "to seek and to save the lost". This study answers the question, *Why?* As well as (surprisingly) why *not*.

⬇ investigate

▶ **Read John 3:1-15** *887*

> **DICTIONARY**
>
> **Pharisee (v 1):** a member of a strict Jewish religious sect.
> **Rabbi (v 2):** teacher.
> **The kingdom of God (v 5):** life under Jesus Christ's perfect rule.
> **Moses (v 14):** Israel's leader during the exodus, when God's people were freed from slavery in Egypt.

2. This Jewish teacher asks a vital question (v 9). What is Jesus' response (v 10-12)? *|'*

3. Jesus claims to be able to speak truthfully about "heavenly things"—but how can he possibly know (v 12-13)?

Jesus looks to the time of Moses in the Old Testament, and likens his mission to an incident during the wilderness years involving a bronze serpent.

4. **Read Numbers 21:4-9.** What was it that caused God's judgment to fall on his people in the wilderness?

129

BECAUSE THEY QUESTIOND WHY HE HAD BROUTHT THEM THERM,

- How did God provide a means of rescue?

HE TOLD MOSES TO MAKE A BRONZE SERPENT.

- What did people have to do in order to be saved?

IF THEY GOT BIT BY A ~~BRONZE~~ SERPENT THEY HAD TO LOOK AT THE BRONZE SERPENT AND THEY WOULD BE SAVED

Just how this incident helps make Jesus' mission of salvation clear is spelled out in the verses that follow.

888

> **Read John 3:16-21**

John 3:16 is so well known that we need to make a deliberate effort in order to read it carefully and in its context.

5. Look at verse 16. Who is the subject of the sentence? In the light of that, who—and what—is this verse primarily about?

> *WHO BELIVES IN JESUS WILL HAVE -ETERNAL LIFE*

6. To whom is the invitation to "believe" issued? (It might help to compare who Jesus speaks to in 3:1-8 and 4:7-10.) Why is this such extraordinarily good news?

281
888

> *IS A INVITATION TO BELIVE IN LOTS OF CULTURES.*

explore more

What does John mean when he talks about "the world"?

886
887

▶ **Read John 1:9-11; 1:29; 2:23-25 and compare with 3:19-20**

In John's Gospel the term "world" is used not to denote the earth so much as the people who inhabit it. How do you think the world, in this sense, would appear in God's eyes?

Taking account of that, how would you describe (from 3:16)...
- *God's love?* ✓
- *God's gift?*
- *God's rescue plan?*
- *God's promise?* ✓

7. Look at verse 17. What was *not* the reason why Jesus came?

> *HE DID NOT SEND HIS SON IN THE WORLD TO ~~NOT~~ CONDEM THE WORLD.*

- Knowing how the world looks to God (v 19-20), does this come as a surprise?

- **Read John 19:30.** In light of John 3;16-17, what was "finished" on the cross? HIS LIFE ON EARTH

8. How does John 3:16-17 connect with the story from Numbers 21? Think about…
- what they/we deserve.

- what God provides for them/us.

- what they/we need to do.

9. What is God's motive in all this?

⊡ **explore more**

optional

God's mission issues from his character: God is a God of love.

▶ **Read Exodus 34:6-7**

This description of God's character is referred to repeatedly throughout the Old Testament (e.g. Numbers 14:18; 2 Chronicles 30:9; Nehemiah 9:17; Psalm 86:15; Joel 2:13).

How do these qualities show themselves in John 3:16-17?

What is the link between God's character and God's mission?

10. What two different responses to God's Son does John describe (v 18-21)? What is the outcome of each?

⤷ apply

John 3:16 is a great verse—but it is a verse mainly about God and his mission. God is the subject of a sentence that summarises the great initiative for salvation that has been taken, and his motivation in doing so.

11. We saw in Isaiah 66 that the goal of God's mission is his glory. We see in John 3 that the motive of his mission is love. What would go wrong in *our view of God* if we lost sight of either one of those?

• What would go wrong in *our approach to world mission* if we lost sight of either one of those?

12. In what ways do Christians sometimes think, speak and act as if God sent his Son to condemn the world?

- What difference would it make in those situations to know that God sent his Son out of love, to save the world?

13. In the light of all that we have read so far, why should we want to engage in God's mission ourselves?

⊡ getting personal

This great verse about God and his mission (John 3:16) mentions a great decision everyone has to take in response to God. There is a lot at stake (see v 18-21). To believe in the Son goes beyond mere intellectual assent. It is to put your trust in Christ's saving work on the cross, just as the people in Moses' day had to look to the bronze serpent in order to live.

If you have believed, then thank God again for his great promise. If not, when would be a better time to do so than right now?

⊡ pray

Give thanks to God for his amazing love and pray for...

- a growing appreciation of the reason for which Jesus came, and a deeper understanding of how God's character drives his mission.

- the people in your locality and nation, who will surely perish unless they believe.

- those nations of the world where it is especially difficult for people to hear the good news of the gospel.

- yourself, to believe—and to go on believing.

4 Acts 1:1-11
THE UNFINISHED TASK

The story so far

God is on a mission to gather a people for himself from every nation and to establish his glory. It's his mission!

Jesus came "to seek and to save the lost" (Luke 19:10). His encounter with Zacchaeus takes us right to the heart of the difference his mission makes.

Out of God's great love, Jesus came into the world to rescue and to save by being lifted up on a cross.

⊕ talkabout

1. Put yourself in the position of a candidate for presidential office on election night—the campaign has been tough and great sacrifices have been made, and now, as the verdict is declared, you hear it announced that you have been elected. What would you think about your task at that moment? Has it been finished, or is it just about to begin? What is the connection between what's gone before and what is about to come?

This study takes us on a leap forward in the Bible's storyline. John's Gospel narrative continues from Jesus' nighttime conversation with Nicodemus to its climax—Jesus' crucifixion. This is the moment when he is "lifted up" to most clearly display God's glory, as he utters his famous words from the cross: "It is finished" (John 19:30).

In this study we'll see how the finished saving work of Christ on the cross leads to the beginning of his task of bringing salvation to the ends of the earth.

⬇ investigate

❱ Read Acts 1:1-8

The book of Acts follows on from Luke's Gospel.

2. Compare Acts 1:1-3 with Luke 1:1-4. If Volume 1 was about "all that Jesus began to do and to teach", what does that imply Volume 2 is about?

3. Jesus' saving work was finished on the cross, but his "job description" went beyond that. **Read Isaiah 49:6.** What great task is God's servant given to accomplish?

- So what remains to be finished in Acts 1:8? How will it be accomplished?

4. What must the disciples wait for before they set out on their mission? Why?

⊡ **explore more**

Acts 2:1-11 describes the fulfilment of Jesus' promise of the Holy Spirit in the remarkable events of the day of Pentecost. So amazing were they that all those who saw and heard them were "perplexed", and asked, "What does this mean?" (Acts 2:12). The apostle Peter says that the key to understanding Pentecost was to be found in the prophet Joel (Acts 2:16-21). In his powerful Pentecost sermon, Peter says that it is the risen and ascended Jesus who will stand as judge on the last day, and he highlights the promise of salvation for all those who call on Jesus' name (Acts 2:22-36).

▶ Read Acts 2:36-41

What was the question the crowd asked Peter next?

What was Peter's response (v 38-40)?

How did this day advance the cause of mission and provide evidence of the ongoing work of Jesus? (v 41).

How does Peter's exposition of the prophet Joel change or deepen your understanding of Pentecost?

What are the implications for us?

5. What is the key question on the minds of the disciples (Acts 1:6)? What do they mean, and why is this so important to them? What is at stake?

6. How does Jesus' response in verse 7-8...
  • put them firmly in their place?

• give them much bigger fish to fry?

7. What does Jesus mean when he says that the disciples will be his "witnesses"? What will this involve for them?

8. If you are familiar with the rest of Acts, can you explain how the disciples get on with the unfinished task outlined in verse 8?

⇥ apply

9. Has the news of Jesus reached "the ends of the earth" yet? Where and who remains unreached?

10. What difference does it make to know that Jesus empowers his witnesses with the Holy Spirit?

getting personal

Jesus is active today, fulfilling his "job description" of bringing salvation to the ends of the earth. Does that excite you? How could you get more on board with this mission?

⊗ **investigate**

▶ **Read Acts 1:9-11**

Acts 1:9-11 records the end of an era. From this point on, Jesus is hidden from sight, as he is taken up into heaven, where to this day he sits at the right hand of the Father, possessing all authority in heaven and on earth (see Daniel 7:13-14).

DICTIONARY

Galilee (v 11): an area in the north of Israel.

11. What is the temptation confronting the disciples, do you think? How do the angels mentioned here react to that?

• In what way is verse 11 a motivation to get on with the work of verse 8?

⊖ **apply**

12. In what ways are we tempted to do the 21st-century equivalent of standing around and staring into heaven?

13. How does what you've read today prompt you to more urgent action?

- What about your church—what place does world mission occupy in its priorities? How is this reflected in your church's prayers and finances?

⬆ pray

Shape your prayers according to the widening circles mentioned in verse 8. Pray for the spread of the gospel in...

- your city or local area.
- your nation.
- the wider world. Choose one or two needy places to focus on.

Pray for your own engagement in mission and that of your church.

5

Acts 10:1 – 11:18
THE GREAT COMMISSION ACCORDING TO PETER

The story so far

Jesus came "to seek and to save the lost" (Luke 19:10). His encounter with Zacchaeus takes us right to the heart of the difference his mission makes.

Out of God's great love, Jesus came into the world to rescue and to save by being lifted up on a cross.

Christ's atoning work on the cross was finished; but his mission to bring salvation to the ends of the earth through the witness of his disciples was only just beginning.

⊕ talkabout

1. When did you last change your mind on something of significance? What was it that brought about the change?

Biblical wisdom says that we need to remain teachable—but all too often we become so attached to our opinions that it is difficult to bring ourselves to see things differently. In this passage the apostle Peter is taught to change his thinking about a fundamental dimension of mission, and given the opportunity to put what he has learned into practice.

⊕ investigate

▶ **Read Acts 10:1-8**

2. What do we discover about Cornelius?

DICTIONARY

Tanner (v 6): leather-maker.

- As a Roman army officer, how would he have been regarded within Israel, do you think?

- How was he viewed from God's perspective?

> **Read Acts 10:9-16**

3. What happened to Peter one lunchtime in Joppa?

4. **Read Leviticus 20:25; Deuteronomy 14:3-8.** In the light of these Scriptures, what would have been so shocking to Peter about the vision he saw and the words he heard?

- Why do you suppose God repeated the vision three times?

Peter was understandably perplexed, until some visitors arrived...

> **Read Acts 10:17-33**

5. What was the result of Peter "thinking about" the vision (v 19, see v 28-29)?

⊳ Read Acts 10:34-43

6. What is the significant change that has occurred in Peter's understanding? How does this affect his presentation of the gospel in Cornelius' home?

⊡ **explore more**

optional

In Acts 10:39 Peter describes Jesus' crucifixion as "hanging … on a tree" (ESV). This appears to be Peter's usual way of speaking of the cross (see Acts 5:30; 1 Peter 2:24, ESV).

Why might this be (compare Deuteronomy 21:23 and Galatians 3:13)? What particular truth does it emphasise?

⊳ Read Acts 10:44-48

7. What similarities do you see between this incident and the description of the day of Pentecost in Acts 2?

• How has God not shown favouritism (Acts 10:34)?

getting personal

"God does not show favouritism." Could the same be said of you and of your church? Is this part of your understanding of what it means to be godly?

→ **apply**

8. "God does not show favouritism." But are there ways in which wrong attitudes limit your engagement in evangelism?

- Peter recognises that these gentiles are authentic brothers and sisters in Christ, who should be baptised as such (v 47-48). Is there anything standing in the way of believers from some kinds of backgrounds being fully accepted and embraced by your church family?

⤓ **investigate**

The parting words of Jesus recorded in Matthew 28:18-20 and Luke 24:46-49 are often called "the Great Commission". Peter's summary of Jesus' words in Acts 10:42-43 constitutes what might be called "the Great Commission according to Peter".

9. Focus on Acts 10:42-43. What is Peter's summary of...

- the message the apostles were commissioned by Jesus to preach (v 42)?

• the core message of the Old Testament prophets (v 43)?

• Is there anything that surprises you in these two summaries?

optional

⊙ explore more

In John's Gospel there is one more version of the Great Commission. "As the Father has sent me, I am sending you," declared Jesus to his disciples. Jesus spoke of sending his disciples on two occasions, first in the Upper Room before his betrayal and again after his resurrection (John 17:18 and 20:21).

❯ Read John 20:21-23

From these verses, what is to be the focus the disciples' mission?

With what authority will they be able to promise forgiveness of sins?

On whom will they be dependent for this work?

What will be the great division their mission will produce? How do you see that playing out today?

❯ Read Acts 11:1-18

10. What impact did Peter's report of the events concerning Cornelius have on the Jerusalem leadership? What conclusion did they draw?

> **DICTIONARY**
>
> **Uncircumcised men (v 3):** non-Jews (Gentiles).

The implication of these events was debated at the Council of Jerusalem (15:1-21), where it was declared that Gentile converts should not be required to become Jews in order to be fully brothers and sisters in Christ. This watershed decision established the principle of the culturally transferable gospel: new believers from other cultures did not need to start dressing like Jews, eating like Jews or undergo Jewish religious practices such as male circumcision. The same is true today. New believers from other cultures do not need to start dressing like foreign Christians, eating like foreign Christians or behaving in a "foreign Christian" way.

🙂 getting personal

Has anything in this study challenged your thinking about mission? Looking back over the first four studies, how has your understanding of mission developed? Have you had your mind changed on any aspect of mission? What difference will that make?

→ apply

11. Peter was immediately given opportunity to apply his new-found understanding in his response to the invitation from Cornelius. What would it mean for you to apply the things you have learned, including any changed opinion or understanding?

↑ pray

For yourself, to be teachable, moulded by God's word and willing to walk in the light of it.

For all those engaging in cross-cultural mission today, especially those known to you or in partnership with your church.

For all theological colleges and mission organisations with responsibility for teaching the theology and practice of mission—that they would be equally committed to being faithful to Scripture and communicating the gospel in a way that "fits" with other cultures.

6

2 Corinthians 2:12-17

THE IMPORTANCE OF BEING SMELLY

The story so far

Out of God's great love, Jesus came into the world to rescue and to save by being lifted up on a cross.

Christ's atoning work on the cross was finished; but his mission to bring salvation to the ends of the earth through the witness of his disciples was only just beginning.

Through a vision from God and an encounter with Cornelius, Peter learned that God wanted him to preach the gospel without partiality or discrimination.

⊕ talkabout

1. Suppose you were about to face an important interview. What would you do in order to impress? Have you ever floundered at an interview as a result of not being properly prepared?

We know we need to try to impress when we go for a job interview— but ought we to try to impress when it comes to presenting the gospel? In this study we look to the apostle Paul as our model missionary. We'll discover that when it comes to the vital task of engaging in mission, Paul thought that it was important to be smelly.

⊕ investigate

> **Read 2 Corinthians 2:12-17**

> **DICTIONARY**
>
> **Aroma (v 14):** smell.
> **Sincerity (v 17):** honestly; without deceit.

In this letter to the church at Corinth the apostle Paul reflects on his recent missionary journey—as he does so, he contrasts himself with the so-called "super apostles" who are now troubling the Corinthian believers.

2. How does Paul regard his experience of engaging in mission (start of v 14)?

"A triumphal procession honoured a victorious general who had been granted the imperium and who had won a just war … [he] sat in a carriage drawn by four white horses clothed in a purple toga [while] a slave held a laurel wreath above his head to remind him of his mortality. At the head of the procession the general's victory was portrayed on paintings … followed by prominent prisoners, then came the carriage of the triumphant general, followed by the troops and the sacrificial animals. At the conclusion of the procession the prominent prisoners were generally executed."

(Eckhard Schnabel, *Paul the Missionary*, page 138)

3. In verse 14, whose victory is being celebrated, and why?

- Who is in the role of prisoner? Why, then, does Paul give "thanks"?

4. In what way does proclaiming the gospel "spread the … knowledge of [God]" (v 14)? (Look back over the previous studies for examples of how this happens.)

- Why might proclaiming the gospel be described as spreading an "aroma"? What does this idea suggest about gospel ministry?

5. What kind of fragrance is the gospel? What does it smell of?

- What two sets of people does Paul distinguish in verses 15-16? Do you recognise this division among people you know?

- How can the same message smell so differently to the two kinds of hearer?

⊡ **explore more**

optional

❯ **Read 1 Corinthians 9:19-23**

In this passage the apostle Paul reminds the Corinthian believers of how he behaved among them when he first brought the gospel to them (see 1 Corinthians 2:1-5).

What is Paul's fundamental aim and ambition (9:19, 22)?

What did this lead him to choose to do (v 20-22)?

How flexible was he willing to be? In what way would this have been costly to someone with Paul's background?

❯ Read 1 Corinthians 10:31 – 11:1

In what way did Paul follow Christ's example? What would be involved for the Corinthians in following Paul's example?

What would this involve for you?

⮡ apply

6. What pressures would we need to resist in order to be properly smelly? Make a list.

7. If people respond negatively, how can we make sure that it really is the gospel that stinks, and not something about our behaviour or approach?

- What additional challenges would working in a cross-cultural situation bring in this regard?

⊡ getting personal

What would it mean for you to be "smelly" among your friends, colleagues or family? Are you willing to be smelly for the sake of the gospel? How might this be to their benefit?

⊕ investigate

> ❯ Re-read 2 Corinthians 2:16-17

8. What is the implied answer to the rhetorical question asked by Paul in verse 16? Why is engaging in mission such a great privilege?

9. What contrast does Paul draw in verse 17?

- Think about the difference between selling a product and speaking on behalf of another person in a situation of conflict—which of these does Paul have in mind as he engages in mission?

⊡ explore more

optional

The apostle Paul did not engage in mission as a lone ranger but always in partnership with others. This involved not only co-workers such as Barnabas, Timothy, Titus, Luke, Epaphras, Apollos, and Priscilla and Aquila but also the churches, not least the believers in Philippi.

> ❯ Read Philippians 1:3-8 and 4:14-20

What form did this partnership take?

What emotional engagement did this partnership involve?

Paul writes of partnership or sharing (*koinonia*) six times in his letter to the Philippians (1:5, 7; 2:1; 3:10; 4:14, 15). The essence of *koinonia* is mutuality in support (each party prays for, cares for and gives to the other) and active engagement (in prayer, in belief, in proclamation, in contending for truth, in suffering for the gospel) in a common cause.

How well does your church's relationship with mission partners express this idea of koinonia? Could it be improved? If so, how could this be done?

⤷ apply

10. What difference would it make to our approach to mission, both personally and as a church, if we…

- thought of ourselves as Christ's prisoners, and not as triumphant generals?

- thought of ourselves as messengers sent by God, and not as salespeople out for our own profit?

⊡ getting personal

Do you view being God's messenger as a privilege? Why/why not? What incentive is there to determine to do this better, and more and more?

⤒ pray

For yourself, to be willing to follow Paul's example in being a humble, distinctive and sincere messenger of the truth.

For Christians facing suffering and persecution simply because their message is an "aroma that brings death".

For God's people throughout the world to be willing to be the fragrance of life and death, whatever the cost.

7 2 Peter 3:1-13
WHAT ON EARTH IS GOD DOING?

15th Dec.

The story so far

Christ's atoning work on the cross was finished; but mission to bring salvation to the ends of the earth through the witness of his disciples was only just beginning.

Through a vision from God, and an encounter with Cornelius, Peter learned that God wanted him to preach the gospel without partiality or discrimination.

The apostle Paul is our model on mission. He saw himself as Christ's prisoner, not an army general; and as a messenger, not a salesperson. His gospel message smelled!

⊕ talkabout

1. "Why is the world in such a mess? Why is there so much suffering and injustice? What on earth is God doing?" Do you, or people you know, ever ask such questions? And if so, why?

⊕ investigate

The New Testament makes it clear that these questions are not new. In fact, they troubled and perplexed believers in the first century, leading the apostles to address them directly. In this passage the apostle Peter does just that, and with this we complete our studies.

▶ Read 2 Peter 3:1-9

> **DICTIONARY**
>
> **The last days (v 3):** the days before Jesus' return.
> **Repentance (v 9):** turning to live God's way.

2.   Why is Peter writing (v 1)? What does he expect his readers to do?

3.   What recurring complaint does Peter anticipate will be heard in "the last days" (the time of Christ's ongoing mission, after Pentecost but prior to his return)? What evidence will be cited in support of it?

- Does this complaint ring true in your experience? What thought process is behind such "scoffing"?

In verses 5-7 Peter refers to the creation account of Genesis 1 and then the story of Noah and the flood from Genesis 6. In both instances he highlights that the sovereign purpose of God was put into effect through his word. First, God spoke the world into being (1:1-27); and second, God spoke words of judgment (see Genesis 6:5-7, fulfilled in 7:1-23). Peter concludes that God's word is powerful and that what God says will, without doubt, come to pass, even if it is sometimes delayed.

4.   What key perspective does Peter want his readers to bear in mind (2 Peter 3:8)?

5.   Why then is God delaying the return of Christ (v 9)?

• What does Peter say is *not* the reason for the delay?

When Christ returns, two things will happen—the day of judgment will arrive (so there will be no further opportunity for repentance), and the new heaven and earth will be ushered in (so there will be no more pain or suffering or injustice for God's people).

Every additional day God allows for people to repent comes at a price: the cost of permitting sin and suffering to persist for another 24 hours in a fallen world.

6. What does God's decision to postpone the return of Christ reveal about his priorities (v 9)?

⤳ apply

7. Is your church using this extra time to focus on calling people to come to repentance? What other things threaten to shift your focus, and steal time and energy for other priorities?

8. God is delaying the return of Christ to maximise the time for mission (and thereby he postpones putting an end to the ills of the world). What implications ought this to have for our priorities as we engage in mission?

⊡ explore more

God's plan and purpose extends beyond "not wanting anyone to perish, but everyone to come to repentance" (3:9). Ultimately, he is working to establish his church, which is the reason why Peter writes his letters. .

> **Read 1 Peter 2:4-10 and Matthew 16:18**

What is the analogy that both Jesus and Peter use for the work of establishing churches?

What does that imply about the work of establishing churches?

Which truth in these verses personally excites you most? How will that shape your attitude as you "do church stuff"?

⊡ investigate

> **Read 2 Peter 3:10-13**

9. What does Peter say is going to happen, in verses 10 and 12-13?

> **DICTIONARY**
>
> **Elements (v 10):** things that make up the physical world: its basic building blocks.
> **Righteousness (v 13):** God's goodness and purity, which will perfectly characterise his people.

- Do you think this is good news? Why/why not?

10. Why does Peter speak of Jesus' second appearing as coming "like a thief" (v 10, see also Matthew 24:36-44)?

How should we live as we look forward to the new heaven and new earth?

Work through Peter's warnings and commands. What portrait of discipleship do they give?

⊡ apply

11. How does Peter say we ought to live in the light of these truths (v 11)?

- What connection does this have with mission? (See 1 Peter 2:12.)

- How have you seen this play out in your life?

12. In what way do the following truths motivate us towards mission?
- The seriousness of God's judgment

- The marvellous prospect of the new heavens and new earth

- Who do you want to share the good news with this week?

⊡ getting personal

"When the gospel takes root in our souls, it impels us out toward the alleviation of all unjust suffering in this age. That is what love does! It [also] awakens us to the horrible reality of eternal suffering in hell, under the wrath of a just and omnipotent God. And it impels us to rescue the perishing, and to warn people to flee from the wrath to come. I plead with you: don't choose between these two truths. Embrace them both. It doesn't mean we all spend our time in the same way—God forbid. But it means we let the Bible define reality and define love."   (John Piper, speaking to the 3rd Lausanne Congress on World Evangelisation, Cape Town, 2010)

How can you speed the coming of the day of God? (2 Peter 3:12)

↑ pray

Thank God for delaying the day of judgment until you had opportunity to respond to his love in Christ. Pray that you would make the most of whatever time is left by proclaiming the gospel to those you know. Pray by name for the individuals about whom you shared in question 12.

Pray that God's church would embrace his mission priorities wholeheartedly and be motivated to proclaim the gospel of his grace urgently.

You might like to finish by praying the Lord's Prayer in the light of these studies.

Mission

LEADER'S GUIDE

Leader's Guide

INTRODUCTION

Leading a Bible study can be a bit like herding cats—everyone has a different idea of what the passage could be about, and a different line of enquiry that they want to pursue. But a good group leader is more than someone who just referees this kind of discussion. You will want to:

- correctly understand and handle the Bible passage. But also…

- encourage and train the people in your group to do this for themselves. Don't fall into the trap of spoon-feeding people by simply passing on the information in the Leader's Guide. Then…

- make sure that no Bible study is finished without everyone knowing how the passage is relevant for them. What changes do you all need to make in the light of the things you have been learning? And finally…

- encourage the group to turn all that has been learned and discussed into prayer.

Your Bible-study group is unique, and you are likely to know better than anyone the capabilities, backgrounds and circumstances of the people you are leading. That's why we've designed these guides with a number of optional features. If they're a quiet bunch, you might want to spend longer on talkabout. If your time is limited, you can choose to skip explore more, or get people to look at these questions at home. Can't get enough of Bible study? Well, some studies have optional extra homework projects. As leader, you can adapt and select the material to the needs of your particular group.

So what's in the Leader's Guide? The main thing that this Leader's Guide will help you to do is to understand the major teaching points in the passage you are studying, and how to apply them. As well as guidance on the questions, the Leader's Guide for each session contains the following important sections:

THE BIG IDEA

One key sentence will give you the main point of the session. This is what you should be aiming to have fixed in people's minds as they leave the Bible study. And it's the point you need to head back towards when the discussion goes off at a tangent.

SUMMARY

An overview of the passage, including plenty of useful historical background information.

OPTIONAL EXTRA

Usually this is an introductory activity that ties in with the main theme of the Bible study, and is designed to "break the ice" at the beginning of a session. Or it may be a "homework project" that people can tackle during the week.

So let's take a look at the various different features of a Good Book Guide:

⊕ talkabout

Each session kicks off with a discussion question, based on the group's opinions or experiences. It's designed to get people talking and thinking in a general way about the main subject of the Bible study.

⬇ investigate

The first thing you and your group need to know is what the Bible passage is about, which is the purpose of these questions. But watch out—people may come up with answers based on their experiences or teaching they have heard in the past, without referring to the passage at all. It's amazing how often we can get through a Bible study without actually looking at the Bible! If you're stuck for an answer, the Leader's Guide contains guidance for questions. These are the answers to direct your group to. This information isn't meant to be read out to people—ideally, you want them to discover these answers from the Bible for themselves. Sometimes there are optional follow-up questions (see ✓ in guidance on questions) to help you help your group get to the answer.

⬚ explore more

These questions generally point people to other relevant parts of the Bible. They are useful for helping your group to see how the passage fits into the "big picture" of the whole Bible. These sections are OPTIONAL—only use them if you have time. Remember that it's better to finish in good time having really grasped one big thing from the passage, than to try and cram everything in.

→ apply

We want to encourage you to spend more time working at application—too often, it is simply tacked on at the end. In the Good Book Guides, apply sections are mixed in with the investigate sections of the study. We hope that people will realise that application is not just an optional extra, but rather, the whole purpose of studying the

Bible. We do Bible study so that our lives can be changed by what we hear from God's word. If you skip the application, the Bible study hasn't achieved its purpose.

These questions draw out practical lessons that we can all learn from the Bible passage. You can review what has been learned so far, and think about practical differences that this should make in our churches and our lives. The group gets the opportunity to talk about what they personally have learned.

⬚ getting personal

These can be done at home, but it is well worth allowing a few moments of quiet reflection during the study for each person to think and pray about specific changes they need to make in their own lives. Why not have a time for reporting back at the beginning of the following session, so that everyone can be encouraged and challenged by one another to make application a priority?

⬆ pray

In Acts 4 v 25-30 the first Christians quoted Psalm 2 as they prayed in response to the persecution of the apostles by the Jewish religious leaders. Today however, it's not as common for Christians to base prayers on the truths of God's word as it once was. As a result, our prayers tend to be weak, superficial and self-centred rather than bold, visionary and God-centred.

The prayer section is based on what has been learned from the Bible passage. How different our prayer times would be if we were genuinely responding to what God has said to us through his word.

1 Isaiah 66:18-24
IT'S GOD'S MISSION

THE BIG IDEA

God declares himself to be on a mission—despite knowing the worst about human sin, he will act to gather a people for himself from every nation and to establish his glory for ever. It's his mission.

SUMMARY

Isaiah was a prophet in the eighth century BC, at a time of serious crisis for God's people. During the reign of four different kings of Judah, he was God's spokesman in Jerusalem, proclaiming a message of warning (of the one true God's anger over sin) and of hope (at the prospect of a coming rescuer). Isaiah's alternating message of judgment and salvation is the central theme of the book, and in the midst of it all, he draws a portrait of the coming Saviour King.

The apostle John writes, "Isaiah … saw Jesus' glory and spoke about him" (John 12:41). In fact, throughout the New Testament, Jesus is identified as fulfilling the promises given by God through the prophet Isaiah, including the ones in chapter 66.

Isaiah's closing vision deserves to be better known than it is, because here God's entire agenda for worldwide mission is spelled out. God has previously declared that his chosen and anointed servant will bring his salvation to "the ends of the earth" (see Isaiah 49:6). Now God sets out his plan and purpose for the world, declaring himself to be on a mission. What is he going to do? How will it be done? Is there a clear strategy? What is the ultimate goal? The answers to all these questions are found in the climax to Isaiah's great prophecy.

Isaiah 66:18-24 sets out God's mission agenda, and establishes the missiological framework for the rest of the Bible. Barry Webb sums up Isaiah 66 like this: "This last, tremendous, paragraph contains God's entire programme for the evangelisation of the world. It is summarised in v 18. In a word, God's fundamental response to the evil actions and imaginations of his creatures is one of grace. His gathering, rescuing activity, once restricted to the dispersed of Israel, is to be extended to all people. He will 'come and gather' people of 'all nations and tongues' so that they may see his glory. The goal of mission is the glory of God, that God might be known and honoured for who he really is. How this goal is to be achieved is spelled out in what follows." (*Bible Speaks Today Commentary*, IVP, p 249-50)

In this study we will focus on three key truths: that God himself is the missioner, that the church is the fruit of his mission, and that its goal is his undisputed glory.

OPTIONAL EXTRA

Option 1: For every study in this series, have one of your group members bring in some information on a particular people group or mission partner to provide a focus for your prayer time.

Option 2: Introduce the theme of this series by dividing your group into teams and having them compete at some fun "missions". Ideas could include these: transferring M&Ms from one bowl to another using chopsticks; throwing a ball round the circle a certain number of times without dropping it; building a tower of paper cups without using hands. Try giving deliberately vague instructions or unclear rules—and watch as chaos ensues! Make the point that whoever is in charge (the missioner) gets to sets the goal, the strategy and the boundaries of the mission—and communicating them is important! Come back to this when you discuss God as the missioner in question 3.

GUIDANCE FOR QUESTIONS

1. What would you want to communicate [about the mission to Mars]? What questions would you anticipate being asked? The root meaning of mission is to be sent somewhere to achieve something. So the idea behind this introductory discussion is to work from an exciting example of a mission in our times (a manned expedition into space) back to God's "mission briefing" in Isaiah 66. In this example, encourage the group to see that it would be important to communicate who is going where, to achieve what, and on whose authority.

2. What precisely is the mission for which the time has arrived (v 18, see also the end of v 19)? By referring back to verse 17, we can see that the "I" in these verses, used three times, is none other than the LORD God. When God speaks, the whole cosmos is required to listen—see Isaiah 1:2. God is going to draw a people to himself. In 66:18 we see that God's mission is first of all centripetal (i.e. drawing in toward the centre)—as with Jesus' great invitation, "Come to me, all you who are weary and burdened, and I will give you rest" (Matthew 11:28). The centrifugal (i.e. throwing outward) nature of mission comes later in this passage (v 19), and is picked up by Jesus in his Great Commission (see Matthew 28:18-20).

- **Who is ultimately responsible for it?** It is fundamental to notice that God is the missioner—it is his mission, not ours. This simple truth has profound implications for how we think and speak of mission, and for what we think we are doing when we engage in mission activity today.

- **What is the scope of this mission?** That Isaiah says the scope of God's mission is "people of all nations and languages" may appear an obvious truth to us—but it was not commonly understood in Isaiah's day. The roots of God's mission go back to his promise to Abraham to bless "all peoples on earth" through him (see Genesis 12:1-3). Isaiah consistently emphasises that this is the scale of God's concern and therefore the scope of his mission (e.g. see Isaiah 2:2-4).

- **What is the fruit of this mission?** The fruit of this mission will be a gathering of people at God's "holy mountain in Jerusalem", where people from the nations are presented as an offering to the Lord. This foreshadows the gathering of God's people at the heavenly new Jerusalem, of which the local church is an outpost (Hebrews 12:22-24). The fruit of mission is the local church.

3. What is the first stage of God's mission plan (v 19a)? In "stage one", God will act to establish the means of salvation—the sign.

- **Who is this "sign"?** Jesus Christ. This will require the historical miracle of Jesus' incarnation as the Servant King and his substitutionary death as Saviour.

- **What in particular about this "sign" will draw people in?** It is through his death that Christ gathers people together.

4. What is the second stage of God's

mission plan (v 19b)?
- **Who will proclaim this message, and where will it be taken?**
- **Where will these people be gathered to, and what will they do (v 20-21)?**

In "stage two", God will commission messengers (the faithful remnant, called here "those who survive") to proclaim that salvation to the ends of the earth, drawing to himself men and women, old and young, from every people and nation, who will constitute his church. As Carl Westermann puts it, this is "the first reference in the Scriptures to mission as we use the term today … that is the taking of a message of salvation to foreign peoples". It is remarkable how this sets the agenda for the entire rest of the Bible.

5. APPLY: What are some of the implications of knowing that...

- **all mission is God's mission?** This demands careful thought, and may require a complete shift in outlook and perspective. Very often mission is assumed to be about what we do, whereas throughout the Scriptures it is what God is doing that is the main thing. He is the missioner, and he is pursuing his mission according to his own plan and timetable. This ought, at the very least, to make us prayerful and humble. We are not in charge—God is!

- **the fruit of mission is the church?** Instead of speaking of "the mission of the church", the Bible attributes the very existence of the church to the fact that God is the missioner. Therefore, when we think of mission, the essential question is not so much "What must I do?" but rather, "What is God doing, and how can I get on board?"

6. What is the ultimate goal of God's

mission (v 22, and also v 18-21)? The ultimate goal of God's mission is to establish his glory—his undisputed, awesome, weighty majesty—something that has been questioned and doubted ever since the rebellion in the Garden of Eden. In fulfilment of God's promise in Genesis 3:15, Jesus entered the world, disclosed his identity (e.g. see John 1:14; 2:11), and went to the cross, which was the ultimate display of God's glory (see John 12:41 and 13:31-32).

7. What would spoil "the new heavens and the new earth"? How does this account for the grotesque vision with which Isaiah finishes? If God's glory is to be established, it must be undisputed. Accomplishing this goal requires that all rebellion be finally put down; otherwise heaven would form merely a suburb of the "new heavens and new earth". Judgment is therefore an indispensable necessity if the goal of God's mission is to be achieved for eternity, as John describes it in Revelation 21:1-8 (see Explore More).

⌄

- **What does this ending teach us about the necessity of judgment and its connection with salvation?** They are inseparable, as God's glory is revealed through both his justice and his mercy—both are necessary. We see this elsewhere in the Bible: for example, with the flood (Genesis 6 – 8), or the crossing of the Red Sea (Exodus 13 – 14).

EXPLORE MORE
What similarities do you see between this passage and Isaiah's closing vision? Why is such a terrible judgment necessary in order for God's glory to be established?

What ought this knowledge prompt us to do? (See Mark 9:42-49 for an example.)
The idea here is to set the study in the context of the Bible's big picture: to show that the twin themes of God's salvation and judgment are something we see repeated throughout. The point is that you can't have one without the other—salvation is always salvation from judgment. The final question prompts us to think about judgement—that having this reality in view ought to make us too take sin very seriously.

8. APPLY: The ultimate goal of God's mission is his glory. How do your goals stack up against his? What difference would adopting God's goal make when it comes to world mission? Note that the goal is not the same as the motive. Throughout the Bible, God's motive for mission is love (as summarised in John 3:16, which we will look at in Study 3). So God's mission is driven by grace, with the ultimate goal of establishing his undisputed glory. Often our own motives are tainted by pride, duty or fear of man. Deep down our goals might be to look good or alleviate a sense of guilt.

9. APPLY: Often we look at the scale and evil of suffering, injustice and oppression in the world and ask, "What on earth is God doing?" What is the answer to that question, according to this passage? The answer, in the light of this passage, is "God is building his church". Whatever else is going on in the world, we can be sure that God is on mission, gathering a people together for his glory. This ought to be a cause of great confidence and rejoicing.

2 Luke 19:1-10
A RICH MAN MADE POOR?

THE BIG IDEA

Jesus declared that the reason he came was "to seek and to save the lost" (v 10)—the story of Jesus' encounter with Zacchaeus takes us right to the heart of the difference his mission makes.

SUMMARY

Luke structures his Gospel around the "coming" and "going" of Jesus, with the pivot in 9:51: "As the time approached for him to be taken up to heaven, Jesus resolutely set out for Jerusalem". By chapter 19 Jesus' journey south from Galilee is almost complete and he stands on the brink of a final week of public ministry before the long-predicted betrayal, trial and condemnation to death by crucifixion. Luke records that Jesus, with his disciples, arrived in the town of Jericho, just a few kilometres from Jerusalem, and he describes a remarkable encounter with a chief tax collector called Zacchaeus.

The story of Zacchaeus is well known to generations of children, not least because of his lack of stature and his tree-climbing ability. But it is intended by Luke as a grown-up's story about one individual's radical repentance and faith. The account concludes with Jesus giving a succinct summary of his mission: "to seek and to save the lost" (v 10). This passage is therefore a highly significant one for Luke's unfolding theology of mission. While Isaiah 66 painted a big picture of God's gathering-in mission, Luke 19 gives us a memorable portrait of how this looks in the life of one person. Jesus seeks out and saves individuals.

The plot unfolds in the town of Jericho. Here

Jesus encounters a wealthy but despised tax collector called Zacchaeus and, to the dismay of the assembled crowd, goes to his house to eat and drink with him as his guest. We're left guessing as to what precisely they talk about—only the outcome of Jesus' conversation with Zacchaeus is spelled out in detail, as the tax collector demonstrates his repentance by relinquishing most of his wealth. Hearing this, Jesus declares him to be a man of faith, a child of Abraham, and rejoices that salvation has come to his house.

The question the careful reader has to decide at the end of this study is whether this is the story of a rich man whom Jesus made poor, or a poor man whom Jesus made rich? On our answer to that question will turn our grasp of Jesus' mission.

OPTIONAL EXTRA

Invite one member of your group to share their testimony at the end of this session. What happened when, like Zacchaeus, they "met" Jesus? What radical change did he bring to their life? Give this person enough notice for them to prepare, and suggest they might like to bring along some photos or objects to help bring their story to life.

GUIDANCE FOR QUESTIONS

1. The doorbell rings, and a stranger stands at the door. What kinds of questions immediately spring to mind? Assuming you felt safe to do this, what would you want to ask? There are no right or wrong answers here. The idea is simply to provoke thinking about Jesus—not only about who he is but why he came.

2. What was on [Jesus'] mind as he headed towards Jerusalem? Jesus has "set his face" towards Jerusalem (9:51), knowing full well that he is walking to his death—and resurrection (18:31-34). If you have access to a map of first-century Palestine, locate Galilee, Jerusalem and Jericho, identifying the journey undertaken by Jesus and the disciples.

3. What kind of person was Zacchaeus? What are we told about him in verses 1-4? Zacchaeus was "vertically challenged" but nonetheless healthy (running, climbing) as well as wealthy (imagine his house, lifestyle, etc.).

4. How would you describe each of these [reactions to Jesus]? What would be the probable reason for each? The reaction of the crowd to Jesus' friendly greeting to the man in the tree was extremely strong. They are incensed that Jesus would go as a guest to Zacchaeus' house, and so they "mutter" openly. By contrast, Zacchaeus' response is immediate and glad—he is overjoyed to have been noticed and accepted by Jesus.

5. How would you sum [Zacchaeus' response] up? The conversation between Jesus and Zacchaeus in his home is not recorded in detail because, it seems, Luke wants his readers to focus on the outcome, both for this individual and for what it demonstrates about Jesus' mission. Zacchaeus' response is radical and unexpected. He promises to give half of his possessions to the poor and repay everyone he's cheated four times the amount.

• **What might Jesus have said to provoke this response, do you think?** Had we been reading through Luke's Gospel from the beginning (as Luke might not unreasonably have expected his readers to do!), we would by now be thoroughly familiar with the consistent message Jesus taught about the seriousness of sin (e.g. 6:46-49), the impossibility of justifying oneself (e.g. 10:25-37), the necessity for his impending death (e.g 9:21-22) and the fundamental importance of making a personal response of repentance and faith (e.g. 16:19-31). All of this renders the radical response that Zacchaeus makes entirely understandable, if unexpected.

• **Imagine you are Zacchaeus' financial advisor: how might you describe his decision?!** From the perspective of a financial advisor, Zacchaeus' decision is crazy!

☒

• **Take a moment to do the maths: what proportion of his wealth would Zacchaeus have had to have obtained fraudulently for him now to be bankrupt?** If Zacchaeus gave away half of his wealth, and promised to repay four times over anyone he had defrauded, he had only to have acquired 1/8 of his income dishonestly to be left bankrupt.

• **Why did Zacchaeus choose not to follow any "sensible" advice, do you think? (What is implied by the manner in which Zacchaeus addresses Jesus?)** Notice that Zacchaeus addressed Jesus as "Lord". He had clearly heard a good deal about him previously, sufficient to make considerable effort not to miss his fleeting visit (v 3). Now he recognised Jesus as his master and responded accordingly—not with reluctance but with enthusiasm.

EXPLORE MORE

Which verb is repeated three times in the passage? How does this explain the prominence of preaching in Jesus' public ministry? Three times the verb "proclaim" is used, emphasising that the central activity of the promised Messiah King will be the proclamation of news.

How does this help us understand what is meant by the descriptions of people in the Nazareth Manifesto? The precise connection between preaching and making the poor rich is not spelled out in Luke 4—on a literal level, this doesn't make sense. Clearly Jesus is speaking in spiritual categories. Later on in the New Testament, the apostle Paul employs these same analogies to describe his gospel ministry, speaking of the gospel as setting prisoners free (see Galatians 3:23-25, 5:1) and "making many rich" (see 2 Corinthians 6:10).

The first thing Jesus says that he came to do is to "bring good news to the poor". How has this played out in Jericho in chapter 19? The puzzle of the Nazareth Manifesto all becomes clear in the Zacchaeus incident as Jesus proclaims the gospel to a "poor" man and leaves him rich beyond measure.

6. What precisely does Jesus say has happened [to Zacchaeus]? Jesus says that "salvation has come to this house" (v 9).

• **With whom does Jesus now associate this changed tax collector? Why is that significant, do you think?** Zacchaeus is declared to be a "son of Abraham". This shows that he too has been made righteous by faith, he is one of God's people, and he is a recipient of these promises too.

7. Looking back over this incident, would you say that this is the story of a rich man made poor? Or a poor man made rich? What difference does this distinction make?** On the answer to this question turns our understanding of Jesus' mission. The fact that Jesus saw Zacchaeus as a poor and needy man (whereas everyone else despised him as rich) reveals Jesus' love for all people and his priorities, preparing us for his mission statement in verse 10. In similar fashion, our answer to this key question will reveal our priorities and, in particular, what we regard as true riches..

8. What is [the purpose for which Jesus came]? Why do you think Jesus said this at that point? Jesus came to seek out and save the spiritually lost and poor—even including people like Zacchaeus.

• **What would it take for Jesus to carry out his mission?** Three times Jesus had prepared the disciples for what awaited him in Jerusalem—his arrest, trial and execution (see Luke 9:21-22; 9:44 and 18:31-34). This indicates that Jesus was fully aware of his impending death, and fully focused on seeing his mission through to its climax at Calvary. It is remarkable that in the closing stages of his journey he paid such careful attention to an individual such as Zacchaeus.

9. In what sense was Zacchaeus lost? He was spiritually lost. **What would it take to...** These questions tease out the consequences of the study. The idea is to carefully consider what is revealed here about the way Jesus saw the world, and the value he placed on each individual—even despised people like a chief tax collector.

• **see people as Jesus saw Zacchaeus?** We need to look beyond wealth or social status and see people's spiritual needs.

Our friends and neighbours might look as if they've "got it all"—but if they have not got the gospel, they haven't got anything of real value.

• **treat people as Jesus treated Zacchaeus?** Ideas might include the importance of focusing on the individual in our evangelism, and being willing to associate with social outcasts at the expense of our own reputation. Who is the equivalent of a despised tax collector in society today?

10. What do Jesus' words in Luke 19:9-10 mean for how we assess poverty and wealth? Are there any implications for our understanding of the scope of mission? It is helpful to pause to think through the implications of this for how we understand human need, and therefore how we pray. For instance, which countries would rate as the neediest in the world if we applied the criteria that categorised Zacchaeus as a poor and lost man? How should this impact our prayers, both privately and in church?

11. If we've been "found" by Jesus, what would it look like to respond with the same heart as Zacchaeus? The significance of his promise of financial restitution is that this represented real repentance for past wrongdoing. We should ask ourselves whether we have taken similar steps to express our repentance in deeds, and not solely in words.

3 John 3:1-21
NOT WHY JESUS CAME

THE BIG IDEA

The world is in rebellion against God and deserves his condemnation—but this was not why Jesus came. Instead, out of God's great love, Jesus came into the world to rescue and to save by being lifted up on a cross.

SUMMARY

John's Gospel has a highly developed theology of mission. From the beginning, John presents Jesus as the one and only Son of the Father, who was sent into the world ("the Word became flesh", John 1:14). Jesus' mission was unique, since he alone came down from heaven and returned to heaven. Yet towards the end of the Gospel, the disciples are sent by him to engage in his mission (John 20:21).

The well-known summary text of John 3:16 was written by John not so much as an evangelistic tool (despite its frequent use as such) but as an explanatory statement of God's initiative for mission. As such, it is not primarily about me or my response to the gospel (important as that undoubtedly is) but about God and his mission. In this study we attempt to read it that way. Although we will read the whole of 3:1-21 for context, we will spend most of the study focused on verses 13-18 (so aim to move through questions 1-3 quite quickly). In Isaiah 66 we saw that the goal of God's mission is his glory; here in John 3 we see that the motive of his mission is love. This is not the mission of an arbitrary dictator but of a good God who longs to save a rebellious world. God's loving character issues forth in his mission to seek and save the lost.

The death of Jesus is central to this study, so it is important that you help your group to home in on this as part of question 8. The choice of the cross as the symbol of the Christian church is both remarkable and shocking. As an instrument of torture, the cross was feared throughout the Roman Empire, where the employment of crucifixion for capital punishment was notoriously used as a deterrent among the subjugated peoples. That alone makes it a bizarre choice—comparable these days to choosing an electric chair or a noose. Why did the followers of Jesus not, for instance, rather choose a stable (symbolising the incarnation) or, perhaps, a dove (symbolising the coming of the Holy Spirit)? John's placing of the death of Jesus at the very centre of his mission provides an important clue as to why the cross was adopted by the early church and has continued to be the symbol of the Christian faith down the ages.

OPTIONAL EXTRA

Bring in prayer letters from mission partners or information on unreached people groups to stimulate your prayer time at the end of this study (see Optional Extra for Study 1).

GUIDANCE FOR QUESTIONS

1. Discuss what you think will happen next. The idea is to focus attention on the task we would expect the deputy head to accomplish, given the authority he or she carries, the scale of the rebellion and the urgent need to protect the vulnerable. We would expect them to curb the riot and punish the wrongdoers.

2. This Jewish teacher asks a vital question (v 9). What is Jesus' response (v 10-12)? The need to be born again is pressed on Nicodemus by Jesus, who uses physical language to speak of spiritual things, much to Nicodemus' bewilderment. This use of metaphorical language is a repeated feature of Jesus' teaching in John's Gospel (e.g. the two waters of John 4 or the two breads of John 6). However, for the purposes of this study, it is important to not let your group get too bogged down in discussing precisely what it means to be born again—the aim of this question is to set verses 14-18 in their context.

3. Jesus claims to be able to speak truthfully about "heavenly things"—but how can he possibly know (v 12-13)? Because he has come from the Father. Another distinctive mark of John's Gospel is John's use of movement language—in his presentation of Jesus' entry into the world, John speaks of his "coming" and "going", and of his "ascending" to return to the Father, having descended from heaven.

☒

• **Why does Jesus speak of himself as "the Son of Man" here, do you think? (See Daniel 7:13-14 and also John 1:14.)** Jesus has come from heaven, but he is also fully man. In the opening section of the Gospel, John speaks of Jesus as the "Logos" (translated "Word") and, having asserted his eternal pre-existence and divine nature, declares that "the Word became flesh and made his dwelling among us" (1:14). Jesus' incarnation happened at a point in space and time, and the disciples were eyewitnesses of his glory. The titles attributed to Jesus in the Gospels include "Christ", meaning the Anointed One or Messiah; the "Son

of God", emphasising his true deity; and here, the "Son of Man", emphasising his incarnation as truly human.

4. Read Numbers 21:4-9. What was it that caused God's judgment to fall on his people in the wilderness? The Israelites were grumbling against God. They were doubting his goodness (which has been at the heart of sin since Genesis 3).
• **How did God provide a means of rescue?** God told Moses to put a bronze snake on a pole.
• **What did people have to do in order to be saved?** The Israelites had to look at it in order to live. Crawling out of your tent in order to look at the bronze snake was an act of faith. Above all, the Israelites needed to believe God's word when he said that looking at the snake would save them from death.

Note: We cannot be certain as to precisely where the quotation of the words of Jesus (opening in v 10) actually finishes and John's own comments begin, because biblical Greek did not use quotation marks. Most commentators reckon that verse 16 onwards is part of John's narrative and that therefore verse 16 constitutes a summary penned by John.

5. Who is the subject of the sentence? In the light of that, who—and what—is this verse primarily about? The subject of the sentence (in other words, the person or thing doing the verb) is God: "God loved … gave". The verse is, therefore, all about him and his activity—not about me and what I should do (although we will come to this in question 8). As such, John 3:16 is one of the great mission texts of the New Testament—it has as its theme God and his great initiative in providing salvation.

6. To whom is the invitation to "believe" issued? (It might help to compare who Jesus speaks to in 3:1-8 and 4:7-10). Why is this such extraordinarily good news? The offer of eternal life is made to "whoever" believes. The two people Jesus encounters on either side of verse 16—a religiously orthodox, influential Jewish man (3:1-8) and a morally compromised, despised Samaritan woman (4:7-10)—represent two vivid examples of the human race. Note that Jesus takes time over each one, and that they are both equally invited to believe.

EXPLORE MORE
How do you think the world, in [John's] sense, would appear in God's eyes? The world is in a state of rebellion against God, it is sinful, and it repeatedly rejects his means of salvation. In other words, it is not particularly loveable!
Taking account of that, how would you describe (from 3:16)…
- **God's love?**
- **God's gift?**
- **God's rescue plan?**
- **God's promise?**
John 3:16 is sometimes said to be the greatest summary text in all the Bible. It speaks of four great things: the greatest love the world has ever seen, the greatest gift the world has ever received, the greatest rescue ever attempted and the greatest promise ever made. It is worth dwelling on each of these in turn in order to see the richness contained within this single text.

7. Look at verse 17. What was *not* the reason why Jesus came? Jesus did not come to condemn the world.

- **Knowing how the world looks to**

God (v 19-20), does this come as a surprise? Given how serious sin is and how widespread its consequences are, we might expect Jesus to have been sent into the world to put down rebellion, sort out the rebels and reassert God's rightful authority (as per the deputy head in our opening question). That this is not why he was sent is truly astonishing—and John's statement helps his readers to grasp this.

- **Read John 19:30. In light of John 3:16-17, what was "finished" on the cross?** Jesus' once-for-all sacrifice to atone for sin—this is the means by which he saves the world. We will return to this thought in the next study when we see that in another sense his mission is not yet "finished"—the task remains to take the news of the forgiveness of sins around the world.

8. How does John 3:16-17 connect with the story from Numbers 21? Think about… "For" (v 16) makes clear that what follows is derived from the comparison that Jesus has just drawn; rather than a new thought, this is a consequence that flows from the nature of Jesus' mission and its similarity to the incident with the bronze serpent in the wilderness.

- **what they/we deserve.** Like the Israelites, we have sinned and deserve his condemnation.

- **what God provides for them/us.** A way to be saved—for us, this is the substitutionary death of Jesus as he was "lifted up" on the cross.

- **what they/we need to do in response.** The Israelites looked to the snake on the pole in faith, believing that through it they would be healed (as God said they would be). Likewise, we must look to Jesus "lifted up" on the cross, and have faith that through his death we will be saved (as God has said we will be). The amazing grace of God provides a way of deliverance and salvation. As John Newton's famous hymn puts it, "Amazing grace! How sweet the sound / That saved a wretch like me! / I once was lost, but now am found / Was blind, but now I see."

9. What is God's motive in all this? This simple question is designed to emphasise the point: God's motive for his mission to the world is love—it flows out of his character as the God of love. It is all too easy to gloss over this. God's love is totally undeserved and his grace truly amazing. See Explore More for more on the link between God's character and his mission.

EXPLORE MORE
How do these qualities [God's loving character] show themselves in John 3:16-17?
What is the link between God's character and God's mission?
From Isaiah 66 (Study 1) we learned that the ultimate goal of God's mission was his glory, and in Luke 19 (Study 2) we have discovered that Jesus declared he came "to seek and to save the lost". Notice how these ideas are brought together in John 3:16-17 and how they begin to come together in a biblical theology of mission. God's mission flows from his character.

10. What two different responses to God's Son does John describe (v 18-21)? What is the outcome of each?
Some people will not believe in God's Son, choosing instead to stay in darkness. They "stand condemned" and will one day face God's judgment. Others will believe in God's Son, accept the truth and come into the light—these are the ones who will receive "eternal life".

11. What would go wrong in *our view of God* if we lost sight of either [God's glory or God's love]? If we lose sight of God's love, then we risk thinking of God as an egotistical megalomaniac, intent on making himself great. If we lose sight of God's glory, we risk "domesticating" him, sidelining him, or assuming that a God of love approves of all the things we ourselves approve of.

• **What would go wrong in *our approach to world mission* if we lost sight of either one of those?** There are lots of answers to this question, so allow your group to explore the avenues of interest to them. If we lose sight of God's love, we risk our approach to world mission becoming callous, uncaring or patronising; we might resort to unloving means to achieve the end we think God wants. If we lose sight of God's glory, mission may become wholly about meeting people's needs, or we may risk becoming discouraged when we face rejection or defeat. Or we'll go about mission for our own glory, in order to make ourselves look and feel good.

12. In what ways do Christians sometimes think, speak and act as if God sent his Son to condemn the world? Your group will no doubt be able to think of various examples known to them, but try to get them to approach this question from a cross-cultural perspective too. For instance, in the past Christians were quick to condemn particular behaviours or customs in other parts of the world. But the message must never be about behaviour modification, but about believing in God's Son as the way to be saved.

- **What difference would it make in those situations to know that God sent his Son out of love, to save the world?** Depending on your group, it might work to role-play conversations between a Christian and a non-believer, in order to demonstrate the difference between speaking out of condemnation and speaking out of love.

13. In the light of all that we have read so far, why should we want to engage in God's mission ourselves? If God's motive is love for the lost (as in Luke 19:10), then true godliness (being like God) demands a corresponding loving concern and determination on our part. This has huge implications for how we look at the world and pray for the needs of the nations. John goes on to speak of the mission of the disciples, and of "those who will believe in me through their message" (John 17:20 onwards). "As the Father sent me, so I am sending you," declared Jesus (John 20:21). This suggests that both Jesus and all his disciples are equally "sent", i.e. chosen and called, set apart and despatched on their respective missions.

4 Acts 1:1-11
THE UNFINISHED TASK

THE BIG IDEA

Jesus' parting words to the disciples show that while Christ's atoning work was finished, his mission to bring salvation to the ends of the earth had only just begun.

SUMMARY

The book of Acts is unique in that Luke is the only one of the four Gospel-writers to pen a sequel. It gives us access to the first thirty years or so of missionary endeavour, as the word of God spread (see Acts 6:7; 12:24; 19:20).

The focus in this chapter is on the unfinished aspect of Christ's work. "It is finished," Jesus cried on the cross, speaking of his atoning work (John 19:30)—yet Luke begins his second volume by speaking of his Gospel as recording "all that Jesus began to do and to teach" (Acts 1:1), with the clear implication that what follows is the ongoing work of the risen Christ. In the opening chapter we hear the parting words of the risen Jesus to the disciples before his ascension, noting that mission lies at the heart of what he says: the disciples are to be Christ's "witnesses", attesting to his death and resurrection in Jerusalem, in all Judea and Samaria, and to the ends of the earth—an unfinished task which continues today. As such, this passage forms part of Christ's commission to every generation in the task of world mission, which is also the focus of the work of the Holy Spirit.

OPTIONAL EXTRA

Finish your study by singing or listening to the hymn "Facing a task unfinished".

GUIDANCE FOR QUESTIONS

1. What would you think about your task [as President] at that moment? Has it been finished, or is it just about to begin? What is the connection between what's gone before and what is about to come? Some tasks simply need to be done—the settling of a bill, the sending of an email; others are never-ending—weeding the garden, cleaning shoes. But there's a third kind of task, where something needs to be achieved first in order to accomplish a longer-term purpose. Such was the death of Jesus on the cross. "It is finished," he cried (John 19:30)—yet Luke begins his second volume by speaking of his Gospel as recording "all that Jesus *began* to do and to teach", with the clear implication that what follows is the ongoing work of the risen Christ.

2. Compare Acts 1:1-3 with Luke 1:1-4. If Volume 1 was about "all that Jesus began to do and to teach", what does that imply Volume 2 is about? Luke's second volume is generally known as the Acts of the Apostles, although in its original form it is titled simply "Acts". Certainly there is much here about what the apostles did after the resurrection and ascension of Jesus. It is also true to say that Luke describes the work of the Holy Spirit, so sometimes Volume 2 is referred to as the Acts of the Holy Spirit. But for Luke, it seems it comprised the acts of the risen and ascended Jesus—it is about all that Jesus continued to do after he had been taken up to heaven.

3. What great task is God's servant given to accomplish [in Isaiah 49:6]?
The servant must become a light to the Gentiles. There is no suggestion here that mission among the Jewish people is to be disregarded or would be a trivial task—the point is, rather, that this servant is too big a figure to be restricted in that way. His agenda is to encompass Israel and also reach beyond to the Gentile nations, even to the ends of the earth.

• **So what remains to be "finished" in Acts 1:8? How will it be accomplished?**
Jesus' unfinished work is to bring salvation to the ends of the earth. This will be accomplished through the witness of his disciples.

⌄

• **What did Jesus do between the resurrection and the ascension? What do you suppose would be the content of the intensive teaching programme mentioned in Acts 1:3? (See Luke 24:13-27, 44-49 for an example).** On the road to Emmaus Jesus led these two disciples in a Bible study, showing how the Old Testament Scriptures not only pointed toward his coming but were being fulfilled in his life, death and resurrection.

4. What must the disciples wait for before they set out on their mission? Why? They must "wait for the gift my Father promised", which is the Holy Spirit. The implication is that this mission cannot be completed by the disciples on their own—the activity of the Holy Spirit is essential. Jesus had taught his disciples this vital truth in the upper room before he died (see John 14:12-14; 14:16-26; 15:4; 15:26-27; 16:7-15).

EXPLORE MORE
[From Acts 2:36-41] What was the question the crowd asked Peter next? What was Peter's response (v 38-40)? How did this day advance the cause of mission and provided evidence of the ongoing work of Jesus? (v 41).
Depending on your group, you may have people with a wide range of opinions on the significance of the day of Pentecost and the meaning of being baptised in the Spirit. The aim of this section is to encourage everyone to park those opinions on one side and listen carefully to the apostle Peter's opinion—after all, he had just emerged from a six-week intensive Bible-training course on these matters led by the risen Jesus (Acts 1:3). The Joel material is likely to be quite unfamiliar to your group. If you have time, it's worth reading through Joel and noticing how he speaks of the certainty of a terrible future judgment (of which the locust storm during his time was a harbinger), and the urgency therefore of not missing the opportunity of the present time to call on the name of the Lord to be saved. Likewise, the disciples know that judgment is coming, and they have been entrusted with proclaiming the promise of salvation before it is too late—hence Peter's impassioned appeal to the crowd in v 38-40. The fact that this message is to be proclaimed to all nations is signified in the miraculous speaking in the native languages of the international gathering on that day.

How does Peter's exposition of the prophet Joel change or deepen your understanding of Pentecost? Everyone is included—men and women, old and young, slave and free. These were the defining categories of Peter's society.

What are the implications of this for us? We are all "Joels" now! That is, we all have a message to speak about future judgment and the present-day opportunity for salvation. This is what it truly means to be a "pentecostal believer"! It is the work of the Holy Spirit to enable us to proclaim that message, even in the face of fierce opposition, as we trust in him to convict people of sin and convince them of truth.

5. What is the key question on the minds of the disciples (Acts 1:6)? What do they mean, and why is this so important to them? What is at stake? The disciples want to know when Jesus is going to restore the kingdom to Israel—i.e. put Israel back on the map as an independent, prosperous and powerful world player. When will the oppression by outside nations (that began with Assyria and Babylon and continues with the Romans) end? The apostle Peter tackles this question in his second extensive teaching sermon, recorded in Acts 3:12-26. Although it lies outside of the scope of this study, you may find that it is relevant to some of the questions that are raised. The key insight that Peter teaches is that the promises of the Old Testament are being fulfilled in two phases (3:18-21). First, God sends the Christ who dies for the forgiveness of sins. Second, Christ returns to restore all things according to the promises set out in the prophets concerning the coming kingdom. This is the same idea we discovered in Study 1 on Isaiah 66, and it places mission in its proper eschatological framework, i.e. between the two comings of Christ. Had Peter grasped this earlier, he would not have suffered the humiliation that occurred at Caesarea Philippi (see Mark 8:27-33). Christ's kingdom has never been about political power as the world knows it.

6. How does Jesus' response in verses 7-8...

- **put them firmly in their place?** Jesus tells them that only the Father knows when the kingdom is going to be restored.
- **give them much bigger fish to fry?** However, the disciples do have an important part to play in the plan. Verse 8 is rightly regarded as a key verse for whole of Acts, as the narrative in the rest of the book follows precisely this order—it tells of the spread of the gospel from Jerusalem to the surrounding areas of Judea and Samaria, and then onwards into the Graeco-Roman world and to the ends of the earth.

7. What does Jesus mean when he says that the disciples will be his "witnesses"? What will this involve for them? A witness sees something happen, and describes what they saw to those who weren't there. In one sense, this makes the task relatively simple. The disciples are not to make up their own message; it's not down to them to devise clever arguments. They just need to faithfully relate what they saw and heard from Jesus.

8. If you are familiar with the rest of Acts, can you explain how the disciples get on with the unfinished task outlined in verse 8? We see believers testifying in Jerusalem (1 – 7), before being scattered to Samaria (8 – 9), then out to Phoenicia, Cyprus and Antioch (9:32 – 12:25), and then from Antioch to Rome (13 – 28).

9. APPLY: Has the news of Jesus reached "the ends of the earth" yet? Where and who remains unreached? Yes and no! Encourage your group both to recognise the remarkable spread of the gospel and to think locally and globally in terms of unreached people groups.

10. APPLY: What difference does it make to know that Jesus empowers his witnesses with the Holy Spirit?
If your group hasn't done the Explore More section, point out from 2:17-21 that the Spirit is given to all believers. This is a huge encouragement when we are afraid or feel overwhelmed at the size of the task. Equally, the knowledge of the Spirit's help challenges us to step out in faith.

11. What is the temptation confronting the disciples, do you think? How do the angels mentioned here react to that? The disciples are caught standing and looking into the sky—where has Jesus gone?! Understandably they are a little dazed and confused, but they have a job to do. Our waiting for Christ's return is to be active, not idle.

• **In what way is verse 11 a motivation to get on with the work of verse 8?**
Jesus hasn't gone for ever, and is coming back. So whether or not we're carrying out his work in the meantime matters (you

could refer your group to the parable of the bags of gold in Matthew 25:14-30).

12. APPLY: In what ways are we tempted to do the 21st-century equivalent of standing around and staring into heaven? Your group may have a variety of different ideas. Could it be that we spend more time talking about mission than we actually spend engaged in mission actvity? If we have our eyes properly fixed on Christ's return, this will spur us into action.

13. APPLY: How does what you've read today prompt you to more urgent action?
• **What about your church—what place does world mission occupy in its priorities? How is this reflected in your church's prayers and finances?**
It is important that the application of this study is not limited to individuals, but includes the local church as God's mission agency.

5 Acts 10:1 – 11:18
THE GREAT COMMISSION ACCORDING TO PETER

THE BIG IDEA

Jesus is both Judge and Saviour—his disciples are commissioned to urge everyone to believe in him, without partiality or discrimination.

SUMMARY

This is a seminal event, so it is no surprise that Luke records the detail three times in Acts (chapters 10, 11 and 15). Its importance lies in the change it wrought in the understanding of the apostle Peter, the miracle of the Gentile Pentecost in the house of Cornelius, and the subsequent lessons determined by the Council of Jerusalem, which set the path for world mission. This study takes in the whole of chapter 10—the aim is to get a grasp of the big narrative, so be sure to keep the first half of the study moving along to ensure there is adequate time for application. We then home in on verses 42-43, which could be described as Peter's version of Jesus' Great Commission. It is one of the great summary texts of the New Testament. The key idea is that God does not show favouritism but invites everyone to believe in him—we likewise must engage in mission without partiality or discrimination.

OPTIONAL EXTRA

If you normally provide refreshments at the start of your study, provide something that looks gross but tastes good (e.g. chopped up Mars or Milky Way bars mixed with jelly, made to look like dog food—put it in an empty dog food can if possible!).

Encourage your group to eat it anyway. Are they prepared to trust you? Or will they be governed by their instincts? Later in the study (question 4), point out that Peter's refusal to eat the unclean animals went beyond squeamishness to a deep religious and cultural conviction.

GUIDANCE FOR QUESTIONS

1. When did you last change your mind on something of significance? What was it that brought about the change? The idea is to get people to reflect on whether they ever change their mind—are they still teachable? Or have they become fixed in their opinions? This is particularly important at this stage of these studies because, as fresh truths emerge from the Scriptures that challenge our understanding of mission, the crunch question is whether we will allow those truths to reshape our thinking and, even, alter our opinions. Such was the challenge Peter encountered one lunchtime in Joppa…

2. What do we discover about Cornelius? He is a Roman centurion, and "devout and God-fearing".

- **As a Roman army officer, how would he have been regarded within Israel?** A centurion was an officer of over a hundred soldiers. As part of the Italian Regiment, he would have been posted to Palestine to play a role in the occupying forces. He would not be popular!

- **How was he viewed from God's perspective?** Favourably, it seems (v 4).

He feared God and lived accordingly (v 2).

3. What happened to Peter one lunchtime in Joppa? Get your group to briefly relate the details of the vision. Note that the roofs of the houses would have been flat, allowing residents to walk on them.

4. Read Leviticus 20:25; Deuteronomy 14:3-8. In the light of these Scriptures, what would have been so shocking to Peter about the vision he saw and the words he heard? God was telling him to kill and eat unclean animals (and therefore break the law that God himself had given).

- **Why do you suppose God repeated the vision three times?** Whether this suggests Peter was slow on the uptake or indicates what a seismic shift this required in Peter's thinking, we do not know—but God shows Peter the vision three times to drive home the point.

5. What was the result of Peter "thinking about" the vision (v 19, see v 28-29)? By accepting the invitation to go to Cornelius' house, and by agreeing to be hosted by this company of Gentiles, Peter demonstrates that he has grasped the point of the vision—it was about much more than the eating of food, and applied to his attitude to other people and involvement in God's mission.

6. What is the significant change that has occurred in Peter's understanding? How does this affect his presentation of the gospel in Cornelius' home? Peter presents the gospel of the forgiveness of sins as being for anyone (v 35) and everyone (v 36). The core message of the gospel is unchanged, but his presentation is adjusted for a Gentile audience who know about

the events of Jesus birth, life, death and resurrection but who are not familiar with the Jewish Scriptures. It is a model of proper contextualisation.

EXPLORE MORE
In Acts 10:39 Peter describes Jesus' crucifixion as "hanging on a tree" (ESV). This appears to be Peter's usual way of speaking of the cross (see Acts 5:30; 1 Peter 2:24, ESV). Why might this be (compare Deuteronomy 21:23 and Galatians 3:13)? What particular truth does it emphasise? Note that in Deuteronomy 21:23 and Galatians 3:13, the NIV uses the word "pole" instead of "tree". In the Scriptures the "curse" is first mentioned as the consequence of Adam's and Eve's rebellion (see Genesis 3:14-19). The biblical language of curse alerts the reader to the seriousness of the problem caused by sin, and to mankind's innate inability to solve the problem. God alone can lift the curse. This he does through Christ's becoming accursed for us on the cross, which will be marvellously demonstrated in the new heaven and earth (see Revelation 22:3).

7. What similarities do you see between this incident and the description of the day of Pentecost in Acts 2? These believers receive the Holy Spirit and start speaking in tongues, just as the believers in Acts 2 did.

- **How has God not shown favouritism (Acts 10:34)?** He has given the same Holy Spirit to Gentile believers as he did to the Jewish believers—both have an equal part to play in his New Testament community, and both have equal equipping for it. There are no second-class citizens in the kingdom of heaven.

- **How has the church worldwide and global mission been adversely affected by Christians who have failed to be godly in this respect?** At times the history of 19th and 20th-century mission was sadly marked by a degree of Western cultural superiority (your group may also be able to think of examples from further back in history). Even today, we're mistaken if we think that the cause of global missions is best served by a "West to the rest" model. In reality God is raising up workers from around the world, some of whom come to "more developed" nations that have a greater need of the gospel.

8. APPLY: "God does not show favouritism." But are there ways in which wrong attitudes limit your engagement in evangelism? Areas to think about might be a reluctance to engage with people of a different class or ethnic or cultural background, or a preference for helping those who are perceived to "deserve" it (as opposed to being in a mess of their own making). Probe your group to consider their attitudes, as well as their actions. Partiality is often seen more in the things we don't do than the things we do.

- **Has history or culture contributed to producing partiality or prejudice? How can the gospel break through such inherited ways of thinking to transform our engagement in mission?**

- **Is there anything standing in the way of believers from some kinds of backgrounds being fully accepted and embraced by your church family?** This question moves things from the area of evangelistic engagement to church fellowship (which is in turn significant for evangelistic engagement). For example, is there an expectation that people need to look or speak a certain way in order to be considered for leadership? There will be an opportunity to return to this thought after question 10.

9. Focus on Acts 10:42-43. What is Peter's summary of...
- **the message the apostles were commissioned by Jesus to preach (v 42)?**
- **the core message of the Old Testament prophets (v 43)?**
- **Is there anything that surprises you in these two summaries?**

The surprising thing here is the way round Peter puts these truths—namely, that Peter's summary of the core message of the New Testament is that Jesus will be our judge (this is the significance of his resurrection—see Acts 17:31), whereas his summary of the core message of the Old Testament prophets is the promise of forgiveness of sins. Many Christians today are under the misguided impression that the Old Testament is all about judgment, whereas the New Testament is all about love and forgiveness. In reality, justice and mercy are twin themes throughout the whole of Scripture. These verses give a fascinating insight into the apostles' understanding of the Scriptures after their six-week tutorial (Acts 1:3) and the essential elements of the gospel they preached. They also tie in closely with the message of Joel as taught by Peter at Pentecost.

EXPLORE MORE
From [John 20:21-23], what is to be the

focus of the disciples' mission? To offer forgiveness of sins.

With what authority will they be able to promise the forgiveness of sins? With Christ's authority.

On whom will they be dependent for this work? The Holy Spirit, who is sent by Christ.

What will be the great division their mission will produce? How do you see that playing out today? Every time the gospel is preached, it divides people into two camps: those who accept the word and receive forgiveness, and those who reject the word and therefore do not receive forgiveness, i.e. the "forgiven" and the "not forgiven".

Some writers have suggested that John's version of the Great Commission (v 21) differs from the others and is more fundamentally important. They read Jesus' words as if they imply "in the same way as"—meaning that the disciples are meant to copy Jesus' "incarnational model" in their own mission. However, it seems much more natural to take Jesus' words to mean that the Son who was sent is now sending his disciples (i.e. the emphasis is not so much on the mode of sending as the fact of being sent). Besides which, the incarnation is presented as being unique in the Gospels, and nowhere is it taught as a model for believers to imitate—instead it is the servant-hearted example of Christ that is to be imitated (see, for example, Philippians 2).

10. What impact did Peter's report of the events concerning Cornelius have on the Jerusalem leadership? What conclusion did they draw? Here we see a teachable open-mindedness on the part of the Jerusalem leadership, who conclude that "to Gentiles God has granted repentance that leads to life" (v 18). Dean Flemming reflects, "Luke's retelling of the tale in Acts 11:1-18 allows the Jerusalem community to catch up with what God is doing. As a result they embrace the unconditional inclusion of the Gentiles into the people of God" (*Contextualization in the New Testament*, p 39).

11. APPLY: What would it mean for you to apply the things you have learned, including any changed opinion or understanding? During the "getting personal" prior to this question refer back to the talkabout question, and encourage people to reflect on their willingness to be taught and changed in their thinking about mission. Make sure they take some time to ponder these things. This chapter is not only about theological understanding (although it certainly is about that) but also about living according to God's agenda for mission. The test for Peter occurs once his visitors issue their invitation—suggest to the group that they think about what it would mean for them to live in accordance with this study.

6 2 Corinthians 2:12-17
THE IMPORTANCE OF BEING SMELLY

THE BIG IDEA

The apostle Paul is to be our example as we engage in God's mission. Instead of being bland company, the Christian is to be noticed for being "smelly"—the aroma, though, will be perceived differently according to who smells it!

SUMMARY

The missionary achievement of the apostle Paul, as recorded in the pages of the New Testament, was truly remarkable.

Roland Allen describes it like this: "In little more than ten years St Paul established the church in four provinces of the [Roman] Empire: Galatia, Macedonia, Achaea, and Asia. Before AD 47 there were no churches in these provinces; in AD 57 St Paul could speak as if his work there was done, and could plan extensive tours into the far west without anxiety lest churches which he had founded might perish in his absence for want of his guidance and support." (*Missionary Methods: St Paul's or Ours?*, p 3)

The book of Acts records three extended missionary journeys undertaken by the apostle Paul and, together with the more autobiographical parts of Paul's epistles (especially the Corinthian correspondence), we possess an intimate account of the missionary endeavours of the apostle to the Gentiles, both in terms of his method and his theology. As such, we have in Paul an example to follow, even as he followed the example of Christ (1 Corinthians 11:1).

In this study we focus on Paul's determination to make an impact for the gospel wherever he went, while personally regarding himself as a prisoner of Christ; and we reflect on what it would mean for us to imitate him.

OPTIONAL EXTRA

Blindfold two or more members of your group and see if they can identify a range of substances by their smell (spices, foodstuffs, flowers, socks). Encourage your volunteers to talk about whether they like each smell or not, and take particular note when they have differing opinions. This is a fun way to introduce the theme of this study, but it should also highlight that different people perceive smells differently and respond in different ways (as with the aroma of Christ in 2 Corinthians 2:16).

GUIDANCE FOR QUESTIONS

1. Suppose you were about to face an important interview. What would you do in order to impress? Have you ever floundered at an interview as a result of not being properly prepared? The idea is to provoke a discussion about the extent to which we try hard to impress others, especially those whose favour we are seeking. This can all too easily lead to cultural assimilation rather than the kind of contextualisation practised by the apostle Paul.

2. How does Paul regard his experience of engaging in mission (start of v 14)?

It's something for which he gives thanks to God—this will need further discussion later on, once it becomes clear quite what it means to be led in a Roman triumphal procession!

3. In verse 14, whose victory is being celebrated, and why?
• Who is in the role of prisoner? Why, then, does Paul give "thanks"?
The startling idea here is that Paul is captive to Jesus. His is the triumph (won on the cross), and now Paul, understanding himself to be a prisoner of Christ, draws the shocking parallel between himself and a captive in a Roman triumphal procession. Far from Paul's missionary journeys consisting of a succession of triumphs, this presents an entirely different picture. (See 1 Corinthians 4:8-13 for Paul's candid account of his experience in the service of Christ.)

4. In what way does proclaiming the gospel "spread the ... knowledge of [God]" (v 14)? (Look back over the previous studies for examples of how this happens.) To share the gospel is to share a message about who God is and what he has done. This needs to be shared from one person to another. For examples from the previous studies, you might go to Isaiah 66:19, John 3:16 or Acts 10:34 and ask, "What knowledge of God is being spread here?".

• Why might proclaiming the gospel be described as spreading an "aroma"? What does this idea suggest about gospel ministry? Imagine walking into a rose garden, with flowers in full bloom. Or passing through the perfume franchise of a large department store. In either case it is impossible to escape the fragrance that fills the air. It is unclear whether the reference

to fragrance and aroma here refers to the incense that was burned during Roman triumphal processions or whether Paul has in mind Old Testament priestly sacrifices. Either way, you can't escape the smell. Schnabel writes, "Whatever the background of Paul's metaphor, it remains true that many people have heard the gospel of God's revelation in Jesus Christ as a result of Paul's missionary work, even though not all the people who have heard believe." (*Paul the Missionary*, p 139)

5. What kind of fragrance is the gospel? What does it smell of? The smell is either sweet or foul—the contrast between a rose garden and an abattoir—and varies according to the spiritual condition of the "smeller".

• What two sets of people does Paul distinguish in verses 15-16? Do you recognise this division among people you know? The two groups are described as those "being saved" and those "perishing", and everyone falls into one category or the other. Note that these are the same two categories envisaged in Jesus' commission in John 20:21-23 (the forgiven and the not forgiven). Again, this is evidence of a uniform theology of mission among the apostles, albeit described in different terms.

• How can the same message smell so differently to the two kinds of hearer? If you hear the message of Christ and reject it, you face death; if you hear the message of Christ and accept it, you receive life. Thus the message produces very different results. But it is also true that the message reveals very different responses. Perhaps you've had the baffling experience of watching two people respond completely differently to the same

evangelistic talk. This passage reassures us that this kind of thing is only to be expected, because we are dealing with eternal realities and spiritual responses.

EXPLORE MORE
What is Paul's fundamental aim and ambition (v 19, 22)?
What did this lead him to choose to do (v 20-22)?
How flexible was he willing to be? In what way would this have been costly to someone with Paul's background? Paul declares himself "free" (see 1 Corinthians 9:1), yet he determines to exercise his freedom in the service of others. He is focused on winning as many people as possible, and in order to do so, he determines to be flexible on all things non-essential (which would have been costly for a Jew such as Paul). This is the essence of the practice of "contextualisation". But this flexibility does not extend to moral ambiguity or doctrinal uncertainty about the truth of the gospel (as 1 Corinthians 5 – 7 makes clear).
In what way did Paul follow Christ's example? What would be involved for the Corinthians in following Paul's example?
What would this involve for you? Paul's imitation of Christ was in self-sacrificial servant-heartedness. It is this attitude that he commends to his friends in the Philippian church (see Philippians 2:1-11), urging them to do likewise. Probe your group to think about ways in which they need to imitate Paul's attitude and example.

6. APPLY: What pressures would we need to resist in order to be properly smelly? Make a list. The answers to this question will vary depending on your group, although the emphasis here should be on the ways in which we are tempted to blend in (e.g. the attraction of a comfortable lifestyle, keeping quiet about the truth of the gospel at work, satisfying expectations from an unbelieving family, conforming to peer pressure at school or college, allowing the ideas of "tolerance" and "equality" to obscure ethical norms and promote moral ambiguity). You might find it helpful to get out a large piece of paper and have people call out ideas.

7. APPLY: If people respond negatively, how can we make sure that it really is the gospel that stinks, and not something about our behaviour or approach? We should consciously examine the way that we think about and speak to other people. Are we speaking from an assumed position of superiority or, in humility, are we drawing alongside them? Are we seeking simply to win an argument or to win over hearts and minds with our love? Do we see people as evangelistic projects or as valued individuals made in the image of God?

- **What additional challenges would working in a cross-cultural situation bring in this regard?** Like Paul, those who are engaging in mission cross-culturally need to contextualise their message. They must show respect for the culture in which they are working— understanding its history, learning its language, appreciating its strengths, dressing appropriately, observing social convention where morally and ethically appropriate for a Christian to do so—in order to win a hearing for the gospel. This can be very challenging to settle into—not to mention costly—but is the distinctively Christian way of serving others, modelled on the example of Christ.

8. What is the implied answer to the rhetorical question asked by Paul in verse 16? Why is engaging in mission such a great privilege? No one is worthy of these things. The stakes are too high, the responsibility too great and the privilege too profound for anyone to take such a role upon themselves—yet the Great Commission lays it upon us all. This should humble us and energise us in equal measure.

9. What contrast does Paul draw in verse 17? Whereas some people "peddle the word of God for profit", Paul speaks "with sincerity"—his conscience is clear as he's not out to profit from his hearers.

- **Think about the difference between selling a product and speaking on behalf of another person in a situation of conflict—which of these does Paul have in mind as he engages in mission?** The way we see ourselves is significant—we are not to think of mission as an exercise in selling a product ("peddlers") but rather, as those who speak of salvation in the name of Christ and in the sight of God.

EXPLORE MORE
What form did this partnership take? What emotional engagement did this partnership involve?
The Greek word *koinonia* is translated variously into English because there is no single equivalent that captures all of its nuances—this obscures how frequently it occurs in the New Testament and especially in the writings of Paul. "Partnership" is probably the closest equivalent term, provided it is understood as active, not passive, and fully mutual rather than a one-way street.
The exercise of gospel partnership helped sustain the apostle Paul throughout the hardships of his missionary endeavours. It is the model given in the New Testament for church relationships with mission partners who are working elsewhere to proclaim the gospel—both the mission partner and the local church are equally engaged in mission (believing the same gospel, proclaiming the same message, contending for the same truths, suffering for the same Lord) but their locations are different. It's not that the Philippian church "supported" Paul so much as they and the apostle supported one another; theirs was truly a partnership in the gospel, evidenced by the warmth of the relationship between them (see 1:3-5 and 4:1). And mission happened as much in Philippi as it did in Paul's groundbreaking ventures elsewhere.

How well does your church's relationship with mission partners express this idea of *koinonia*? Could it be improved? If so, how? Allow your group to discuss their ideas. For example, could you send your mission partners prayer requests from your church to increase the sense of a two-way partnership?

10. APPLY: What difference would it make to our approach to mission, both personally and as a church, if we...

- **thought of ourselves as Christ's prisoners, and not as triumphant generals?** Belonging to him means we won't secretly measure ourselves up against others to see who is best at evangelism—because we're all prisoners together. We would be humble in our approach to others, not holding ourselves up to be anything special. And we would be prepared to do unseen, difficult or downright unpleasant tasks for the sake of the gospel.

- **thought of ourselves as messengers**

sent by God, and not as salespeople out for our own profit? There are lots of directions this discussion could be taken in. For example, we would invest in others relationally, because we're not just looking for a quick win. We would not focus only on those who appear "strategic" or impressive in some way, but would readily share the gospel message with whoever we can. And we would be more confident in doing that because we're not driven by sales targets—what we have to do is faithfully deliver the message and pray for God's activity in the hearers' hearts and minds.

7

2 Peter 3:1-13

WHAT ON EARTH IS GOD DOING?

THE BIG IDEA

God is delaying the day of the Lord—when he will put an end to this world's rebellion, and to the suffering in it—in order to fulfil his mission agenda.

SUMMARY

In this concluding section of his second letter, the apostle Peter spells out the answer to one of the biggest theological conundrums at the heart of mission: why hasn't Jesus come back yet? Given all the suffering in the world, what is he waiting for?

In this passage Peter acknowledges the delay in the coming of the kingdom and sets out God's mission agenda as the overriding consideration determining his timetable. God is patiently waiting for more people to respond to the gospel message with repentance. Recalling the question the eleven disciples posed to Jesus after his resurrection and Jesus' reply, "It is not for you to know the times or dates the Father has set by his own authority" (Acts 1:6-7), it seems probable that Peter owes this explanation to Jesus' six-week tutorial on the kingdom of God. This study call us to grasp seriously the prospect of judgment and to respond by engaging in urgent mission.

OPTIONAL EXTRA

Describe the following two scenes, and then see if your group guess what is going on:

A grown man is standing alone in front of a large building. In his hands are two objects that look like oversize table-tennis bats. He is wearing a brightly coloured jacket and what appear to be headphones. Standing still, he holds his arms up high and begins waving the bats, slowly and deliberately. What on earth is he doing?

The date is April 15th, 1912. In the North Atlantic Ocean, in the darkness of night, a huge, multi-funnelled ship is listing, having suffered catastrophic damage to its hull from a collision with an iceberg. The ship is sinking, lifeboats are being launched and passengers are scrambling to get into them. Meanwhile, on the main deck, a group of eight musicians are calmly playing through some well-known Christian hymns. What on earth do they think they are doing?

If you have time, invite your group to make up their own scenes. Afterwards, analyse how you got to your answers. What additional knowledge did you draw upon? Did some members of the group find the scene easier to understand than others? Why? Were there any elements missing from the description? And, if so, how would their inclusion have helped? The point to make is that the bigger picture enables us to make sense of the scenes imagined.

GUIDANCE FOR QUESTIONS

1. "What on earth is God doing?" Do you, or people you know, ever ask such questions? And if so, why? Allow your group to share their answers. Often it is when we see or experience grief, suffering, oppression, cruelty and need that we question what God is doing. When engaging with non-believers evangelistically, most of us have come up against comments such as "If God really is God, he must realise how bad things are in the world—so, why doesn't he do something about it?"

2. Why is Peter writing (v 1)? What does he expect his readers to do? Peter wants to remind his Christian readers of what they already know from the Old Testament and the teaching of the apostles. Likewise, what we read in this study might not be new to us, but we constantly need to be helped towards "wholesome thinking"! Note the emphasis on the mind. This is a constant feature of Peter's writing (see 1 Peter 1:13; 2:19; 3:8; 4:1, 7; 5:8).

3. What recurring complaint does Peter anticipate will be heard in "the last days" (the time of Christ's ongoing mission, after Pentecost but prior to his return)? What evidence will be cited in support of it? See Acts 2 for Peter's understanding of the "last days" (study 4). The accusation is that nothing has changed in the world and therefore Jesus was not who he said he was. This is a reason sometimes cited by those familiar with the Old Testament Scriptures to dismiss the possibility that Jesus of Nazareth was God's Messiah. Some years ago a leading rabbi in an interview at Christmas time on BBC radio put it like this: "The Old Testament prophets—especially Isaiah—teach that when Messiah comes the whole world will be transformed with sickness and disease abolished, conflicts resolved and peace reigning. But when we look around the world, this simply has not happened. Therefore, however wonderful a man Jesus was, and whatever miracles he performed, the one thing we know is that he was not God's promised Messiah."

• **Does this complaint ring true in your experience?** Use this question to link back to the things shared at the start of the study. **What thought process is behind such "scoffing"?** These scoffers ignore ("deliberately forget") the power of God's word (see note in the Study Guide on verses 5-7). Now, as then, when God says something will happen, it will happen. This great truth is found, and emphasised, in Isaiah 55:10-11. Here the prophet declares that God's word not only informs (by teaching and revealing truth); it also performs (accomplishing God's sovereign purposes), and the effect of rain on parched land is a vivid illustration of this.

4. What key perspective does Peter want his readers to bear in mind (2 Peter 3:8)? God does not relate to time as we do. He is the Creator of it and therefore stands outside of it. God sees more intensively than we do (so 24 hours is spread out as if it lasts 1000 years) and more extensively (so that 1000 years is but a day to him who is eternal).

5. Why then is God delaying the return of Christ (v 9)?
• **What does Peter say is *not* the reason for the delay?**
This is an important step in Peter's argument, so work hard to help people grasp both the "not" and the "but" aspects. It's not that God is slow or forgetful or unable, but rather, that he has another, overriding priority that determines the choice he makes. It is a positive choice on God's part to delay judgment day in order to maximise the time for mission and give further opportunities for people to "come to repentance", but that delay will not be for ever.

6. What does God's decision to postpone the return of Christ reveal about his priorities (v 9)? This is a cosmic trade-off—just as an employer may allow employees to purchase additional days of annual leave by forgoing some salary, additional days for mission come at a price: the terrible cost of permitting sin and suffering to persist for another 24 hours in a fallen world, which requires "patience" on his part. The question is this: how important is that additional day? And is it worth the cost? This verse reveals that God's greatest priority is that people might be saved from "perishing"—the eternal death that awaits those who do not repent in time.

7. APPLY: Is your church using this extra time to focus on calling people to come to repentance? What other things threaten to shift your focus, and steal time and energy for other priorities? Answers might include an emphasis on anything that may be good in itself but isn't prioritising mission e.g. a preoccupation with issues of climate change or social justice at the expense of gospel proclamation. In other words, focusing on the problems of a fallen world rather than proclaiming and sharing the solution which is the gospel of Christ.

8. APPLY: God is delaying the return of Christ to maximise the time for mission (and thereby he postpones putting an end to the ills of the world). What implications ought this to have on our priorities as we engage in mission? If God postpones putting an end to the economic and social ills of the world in order to make extra time for mission, it makes no sense for his church to spend that extra time focusing on the economic and social ills of the world, rather than calling people to "come to repentance" (v 9). That is not

to say that mercy ministries (such as medical missions, education projects, work with abuse victims, etc.) are unimportant—but they must at some stage be accompanied by gospel proclamation and an invitation to repent and believe the good news.

EXPLORE MORE
Read 1 Peter 2:4-10 and Matthew 16:18. What analogy do Jesus and Peter use for the work of establishing churches? The work is likened to building. Paul also employs the building analogy in 1 Corinthians 3:10-11 and Ephesians 2:19-22. **What does that imply about the work of establishing churches?** Although we might be familiar with the vocabulary of "church planting", in New Testament language it is never the church which is "planted"—what is planted is the seed of the gospel which, when it falls into good soil, germinates and produces believers (see Mark 4:1-20 and 1 Corinthians 3:6-7). These believers must then be built as "living stones" into church (note how Paul switches analogy from sowing to building in 1 Corinthians 3:9). This is not mere semantics, because analogies matter—they fashion our thinking, and from them we draw implications. Thus to muddle analogies is to invite the wrong inferences to be drawn. Note that it is on the foundation of Christ that the church is built. **Which truth in these verses personally excites you most? How will that shape your attitude as you "do church stuff"?** Allow your group to share what has struck them. The idea is simply to refresh our vision of the church as the agent of God's mission, and encourage us to all play our part in it.

9. What does Peter say is going to happen, in verses 10 and 12-13? The present earth and heaven will be destroyed and a new heaven and a new earth will be established. The question of what is meant by "a new heaven and a new earth" is debated. Clearly a great deal changes, which implies discontinuity, but to what extent will there also be continuity? In other words, is this world simply renewed or are we expecting a wholly new cosmos? These are questions that are beyond the scope of this study, although in truth the word "new" implies both continuity and discontinuity. (For instance, in order for a "new coat" to be a new coat, it must still be a coat, not something entirely different altogether.) **Note:** Some of your group may have questions about verse 12. How do we "speed" the coming of Christ's return? We do this through our obedience, prayer and witness. This is not the only place in the New Testament where this idea is found—the prayer "Your kingdom come" is an appeal for God to bring about his kingdom in its fullness, but it is also a commitment to live obediently in the meantime. Matthew 24:14 tells us that this present age will last for as long as it takes for all God's elect to be reached with the gospel message—in this sense we speed Christ's coming as we tell others about him, and as they respond with repentance and faith.

- **Do you think this is good news? Why/ why not?** This is great news for those who belong to Christ. It is something we can "look forward" to (v 13). The new heavens and earth will be "where righteousness dwells"—it will be a wonderful place to be. But this is not good news for those who have not repented and turned to Christ. All their sin will be "laid bare" (v 10)—a terrifying prospect for those not under the protection of Christ's atonement—and like those living in the time of the flood, through God's judgment the ungodly will face "destruction" (v 7).

10. Why does Peter speak of Jesus' second appearing as coming "like a thief"? (v 10, see also Matthew 24:36-44). Although Jesus' second coming is promised, it will nonetheless be sudden and at a time which we do not expect. Since we don't know when it will be, it is important to be ready at all times.

EXPLORE MORE
Read 2 Peter 3:14-18
How should we live as we look forward to the new heaven and new earth? Work through Peter's warnings and commands. What portrait of discipleship do they give?
We are to "make every effort to be found spotless, blameless and at peace with [God]" (v 14). This is about being sure to continue in repentance and faith, and not somehow trying to "earn" peace with God through our efforts. We need to be on our guard against false teachers, including those who say that the way we live doesn't matter (v 17). We ought to be seeking to grow in our knowledge of Christ, and in gracious, Christ-like character (v 18). Thus discipleship, as we wait for Christ's return, is not passive or static—it is something that is active, intentional and ever-deepening.

11. How does Peter say we ought to live in the light of these truths (v 11)? Peter says that the application of this truth is to seek to "live holy and godly lives" (v 11).

- **What connection does this have with mission? (See 1 Peter 2:12.)** 1 Peter 2:12 shows us that the way we live is an important part of our witness. See also 1 Peter 3:1-2: our godly behaviour ought to commend the gospel message.

- **How have you seen this play out in your life?** Encourage your group to share stories of people who were first attracted to Christianity by the lives of the Christians they knew.

12. In what way do the following truths motivate us towards mission?
- **The seriousness of God's judgment**
- **The wonderfulness of the new heavens and earth**
- **Who do you want to share the good news with this week?**

This is an opportunity to round up the key things covered in this session, and to encourage people to put them into action. Invite each group member to name at least one person who they want to share the gospel with. Make sure to pray for these people at the end of the session, and to check in with each other later in the week to see how God has been answering prayer and providing opportunities.

AUTHOR'S ACKNOWLEDGEMENTS

These studies have been shaped by three streams of influence: multiple gospel partners within BCMS Crosslinks, both at home and abroad, over 13 years of labouring together to take God's word to God's world; my personal endeavours to get to grips with the biblical theology of mission by studying the Scriptures afresh with the help of many writers and biblical scholars; and the generous opportunities afforded to me to preach and teach on this most glorious of themes in churches and conferences around this country, elsewhere in Europe and among the churches and student Christian movements in various parts of Africa.

In particular my thanks are due to Mark Gillespie, Tim Houghton, John Martin and Gemma Milnes, who encouraged and helped develop the early drafts of this material; to Rachel Jones of The Good Book Company; and to my senior colleagues Andy Lines, Giles Rawlinson and Jo Sayer for their example, fellowship and stimulus. They are not, of course, responsible for the deficiencies that remain, but without their contribution these studies would never have seen the light of day. *Soli Deo Gloria.*

BCMS
Crosslinks

Crosslinks exists to help people get involved in God's mission. We believe every Christian has a part to play in God's plan for the world.

Crosslinks has workers in more than 35 countries worldwide. Over 130 of these are long-term mission partners sent by churches in Britain and Ireland. We also help indigenous workers run gospel projects in their home nations, and we provide bursaries to enable those in less well-off countries to study for ministry. In addition, Crosslinks has a short-term programme sending men and women to serve across the globe. All Crosslinks workers are engaged in word ministry, with the Bible at the forefront of what they do.

Get involved today at
www.crosslinks.org

Good Book Guides
for groups and individuals

Judges: The flawed and the flawless

Timothy Keller
Senior Pastor, Redeemer Presbyterian Church, Manhattan

Welcome to a time when God's people were deeply flawed, often failing and struggling to live in a world which worshipped other gods. Our world is not so different—we need Judges to equip us to live for God in our day, and remind us that he is a God of patience and mercy.
Also by Tim Keller: Romans 1–7; Romans 8–16; Galatians

Daniel: Staying strong in a hostile world

David Helm
Lead Pastor, Holy Trinity Church, Chicago

The first half of Daniel is well known and much loved. The second is little read and less understood! David Helm leads groups through the whole book, showing how the truths about God in the second half enabled Daniel and his friends—and will inspire us—to live faithful, courageous lives.

Esther: Royal rescue

Jane McNabb
Chair of the London Women's Convention

The experience of God's people in Esther's day helps us in those moments when we question God's sovereignty, his love or his faithfulness. Their story reveals that despite appearances, God is in control, and he answers his people's prayers—often in most unexpected ways.

Now nearly 60 titles in the range. Visit:
www.thegoodbook.co.uk/goodbookguides

1 Corinthians 1–9: Challenging church

Mark Dever
Senior Pastor, Capitol Hill Baptist Church, Washington DC; President, 9Marks Ministries

The church in Corinth was full of life, and just as full of problems. As you read how Paul challenges these Christians, you'll see how you can contribute to your own church becoming truly shaped by the gospel.

Also by Mark Dever: 1 Corinthians 10–16

James: Genuine faith

Sam Allberry
Speaker, Ravi Zacharias International Ministries

Many Christians long for a deeper, more whole-hearted Christian life. But what does that look like? This deeply practical letter was written to show us, and will reveal how to experience joy in hardships, patience in suffering and wholeheartedness in how we speak, act and pray.

Also by Sam Allberry: Man of God / Biblical Manhood

1 Peter: Living well on the way home

Juan Sanchez
Preaching Pastor, High Pointe Baptist Church, Austin, Texas

The Christian life, lived well, is not easy—because we don't belong in this world. Learn from Peter how to journey on rather than retreat, and to do so with joy and hope, rather than gritted teeth.

thegoodbook
COMPANY

Good Book Guides
The full range

2 Corinthians 8–13:
7 Studies
James Hughes
ISBN: 9781784981266

Galatians: 7 Studies
Timothy Keller
ISBN: 9781908762566

Ephesians: 10 Studies
Thabiti Anyabwile
ISBN: 9781907377099

Ephesians: 8 Studies
Richard Coekin
ISBN: 9781910307694

Philippians: 7 Studies
Steven J. Lawson
ISBN: 9781784981181

Colossians: 6 Studies
Mark Meynell
ISBN: 9781906334246

1 Thessalonians:
7 Studies
Mark Wallace
ISBN: 9781904889533

1 & 2 Timothy: 7 Studies
Phillip Jensen
ISBN: 9781784980191

Titus: 5 Studies
Tim Chester
ISBN: 9781909919631

Hebrews: 8 Studies
Justin Buzzard
ISBN: 9781906334420

James: 6 Studies
Sam Allberry
ISBN: 9781910307816

1 Peter: 6 Studies
Juan R. Sanchez
ISBN: 9781784980177

1 John: 7 Studies
Nathan Buttery
ISBN: 9781904889953

Revelation: 7 Studies
Tim Chester
ISBN: 9781910307021

TOPICAL

Man of God: 10 Studies
Anthony Bewes & Sam
Allberry
ISBN: 9781904889977

Biblical Womanhood:
10 Studies
Sarah Collins
ISBN: 9781907377532

The Apostles' Creed:
10 Studies
Tim Chester
ISBN: 9781905564415

**Promises Kept Bible
Overview:** 9 Studies
Carl Laferton
ISBN: 9781908317933

Contentment: 6 Studies
Anne Woodcock
ISBN: 9781905564668

**These truths alone: the
Reformation Solas**
6 Studies
Jason Helopoulos
ISBN: 9781784981501

Women of Faith:
8 Studies
Mary Davis
ISBN: 9781904889526

Meeting Jesus: 8 Studies
Jenna Kavonic
ISBN: 9781905564460

Heaven: 6 Studies
Andy Telfer
ISBN: 9781909919457

Making Work Work:
8 Studies
Marcus Nodder
ISBN: 9781908762894

The Holy Spirit: 8 Studies
Pete & Anne Woodcock
ISBN: 9781905564217

Experiencing God:
6 Studies
Tim Chester
ISBN: 9781906334437

Real Prayer: 7 Studies
Anne Woodcock
ISBN: 9781910307595

COMPANY

BIBLICAL | RELEVANT | ACCESSIBLE

At The Good Book Company, we are dedicated to helping Christians and local churches grow. We believe that God's growth process always starts with hearing clearly what he has said to us through his timeless word—the Bible.

Ever since we opened our doors in 1991, we have been striving to produce Bible-based resources that bring glory to God. We have grown to become an international provider of user-friendly resources to the Christian community, with believers of all backgrounds and denominations using our books, Bible studies, devotionals, evangelistic resources, and DVD-based courses.

We want to equip ordinary Christians to live for Christ day by day, and churches to grow in their knowledge of God, their love for one another, and the effectiveness of their outreach.

Call us for a discussion of your needs or visit one of our local websites for more information on the resources and services we provide.

Your friends at The Good Book Company

thegoodbook.com | thegoodbook.co.uk
thegoodbook.com.au | thegoodbook.co.nz
thegoodbook.co.in